The Organized Teacher's Guide to
Classroom Management

Steve Springer, M.A.,
and
Kimberly Persiani, Ed.D.

Mc
Graw
Hill

New York   Chicago   San Francisco   Lisbon   London   Madrid   Mexico City
Milan   New Delhi   San Juan   Seoul   Singapore   Sydney   Toronto

The **McGraw·Hill** Companies

Copyright © 2011 by The McGraw-Hill Companies, Inc. All rights reserved. Printed in
the United States of America. Except as permitted under the United States Copyright Act
of 1976, no part of this publication may be reproduced or distributed in any form or by
any means, or stored in a database or retrieval system, without the prior written
permission of the publisher.

7 8 9 10 11 12 QVS/QVS 20 19 18 17 16

ISBN   978-0-07-174198-9 (book and CD set)
MHID   0-07-174198-4

ISBN   978-0-07-174200-9 (book alone)
MHID   0-07-174200-X

e-ISBN 978-0-07-174508-6
e-MHID 0-07-174508-4

Library of Congress Control Number   2010936008

Interior design by Village Bookworks, Inc.
Interior and cover illustrations by Steve Springer

McGraw-Hill books are available at special quantity discounts to use as premiums and
sales promotions or for use in corporate training programs. To contact a representative,
please e-mail us at bulksales@mcgraw-hill.com.

This book is printed on acid-free paper.

CD-ROM Instructions

For PC:

This disk will start automatically or will prompt you to "Run autorun.exe." If it does not,
open My Computer and double-click on "Classroom Management" in your CD-ROM
drive; then double-click on "autorun.exe." This will bring up the book cover; click this to
access the Table of Contents, which contains links to more than 50 printable PDFs, many
of which are also available in fill-in format.

For Mac:

Insert the CD-ROM into your CD-ROM drive. A window will open with the contents of the
CD-ROM. Double-click on "autorun.exe." This will bring up the book cover; click this to
access the Table of Contents, which contains links to more than 50 printable PDFs, many
of which are also available in fill-in format.

Contents

3 Establishing Rules, Consequences, and Procedures *65*

4 Managing Student Behavior 85

5 Getting Off to a Good Start 103

6   Know Your Support Team   *127*

7   Planning, Instruction, and Assessment   *145*

8 Managing Active Learning *173*

9 Instructional Challenges *191*

10 Curriculum Overview *213*

What Do Teachers Make?

The dinner guests were sitting around the table, discussing life.

One man, a CEO, decided to explain the problem with education. He argued, "What's a kid going to learn from someone who decided his best option in life was to become a teacher?"

To prove his point, he turned to one of the guests and said, "You're a teacher, Bonnie. Be honest. What do you make?"

Bonnie, who had a reputation for honesty and frankness, replied, "You want to know what I make?" She paused for a second, then began . . .

"Well, I make kids work harder than they ever thought they could.

"I make a C+ kid feel like a Congressional Medal of Honor winner.

"I make kids sit through 40 minutes of class time when their parents can't make them sit still for five minutes without an iPod, GameCube, or movie on TV.

"You want to know what I make?" Bonnie asked again. She paused and looked at every person at the table, then continued . . .

"I make kids wonder.

"I make them question.

"I make them apologize and mean it.

"I make them have respect and take responsibility for their actions.

"I teach them to write, and then I make them write—keyboarding isn't everything.

"I make them read, read, read.

"I make them show all their work in math. They use their God-given brains, not their man-made calculators.

"I make students from other countries learn everything they need to know about English while preserving their unique cultural identity.

"I make my classroom a place where all my students feel safe.

"I make my students stand, place their hands over their hearts, and say the Pledge of Allegiance, because we live in the United States of America.

"Finally, I make them understand that if they use the gifts they were given, work hard, and follow their hearts, they can succeed in life."

Bonnie paused one last time, then continued . . .

"Then, when people try to judge me by what I make, with me knowing money isn't everything, I can hold my head up high and pay no attention—because they are ignorant.

"You want to know what I make? **I make a difference.** What do you make, Mr. CEO?"

The man's jaw dropped. He was at a complete loss for words.

◆ ◆ ◆

Teachers *do* make a difference. When you are having "one of those days" or you don't think you are paid enough, read this story to yourself.

Circulated via e-mail; author unknown

Preface

Why is this story so important? Well, when Steve and I went through our teacher education programs, we were both cognizant of the fact that since we would be teaching other people's children, we would have a tremendous amount of responsibility in our jobs. However, when we were teacher candidates going through our studies and practicum—and hoping for a teaching position—our response when people asked what we did for a living was, "I'm just a teacher."

The teaching profession has always been a passion for those of us who take it on, but even some of the most seasoned teachers fall into the trap of thinking their career choice is "less than," often because they aren't held in high regard by the community at large.

In the last several years, many of us who mentor new teachers have tried hard to get them to understand that they have an enormous responsibility in teaching children and that this is a privilege that they should embrace with great zeal. There is never a time when teachers who work hard to plan, instruct, assess, and love their students should ever feel that they are "just a teacher."

This book is meant to provide teachers with a clear and practical resource for organizing and managing a classroom. We want you to have every opportunity to meet the responsibility that you have committed your time and heart to. We want you to be able to take everything you learned in your credential program and everything you have reviewed in professional developments in your district and put them to use in realistic ways. This book will help you do that. It's a one-stop resource for planning, instruction, motivation, rules and consequences, discipline, assessment, parent involvement, and much more.

As you engage with this book, remember that students are coming into schools with more diverse backgrounds, ability levels, interests, and special needs than at any other time in history. Lesson preparation, instruction, assessment, and discipline have taken on an entirely new dimension, due to the many variables present in today's classroom. To manage your classroom well, you must know your students, their backgrounds, and their families, and you must have a clear idea about how you will make your classroom run smoothly.

Steve and I have tried to make this book useful and practical by providing numerous templates and organizing ideas. Much of what you will find in this book is influenced by our own experiences as classroom teachers, mentors, adult educators in credential programs, and conference presenters. The teachers we have come into contact with in the last couple of years have helped us understand what they would like to see in a book such as this. We have included overviews of classroom management theories, age- and grade-level profiles of students, and curriculum by subject area. We hope it will serve you well.

Kimberly Persiani

A NOTE TO THE TEACHER

 This CD icon is used in the text margin of this book to direct you to a template on the accompanying CD that relates to the text.

1 Theorists

Consider the ways in which you might incorporate discipline, planning, and student engagement into your classroom management. This chapter presents several theorists' approaches to discipline as a part of classroom management. Explore these approaches, and then do your own research to come up with a combination of discipline styles, planning, and student engagement that works best for you.

How you discipline your students, manage your classroom, deliver instruction, and model and demonstrate lessons for your students are all based on the work of educational theorists. The following are only a few of the many popular theorists who offer effective ideas about designing instruction, creating a democratic classroom, and providing a safe and welcoming environment for your students. Only you can decide which theorists you identify most closely with, but once you have determined that, you will be one step closer to having a classroom that runs smoothly, is based on respect and responsibility, and is more student centered.

Ten Theorists of Classroom Management

Theorist	Approach
Lee and Marlene Canter	Assertive Discipline
Richard Curwin and Allen Mendler	Discipline with Dignity
Rudolph Dreikurs	Discipline Through Democratic Teaching
Haim Ginott	Discipline Through Congruent Communication
William Glasser	Noncoercive Discipline
Fred Jones	Positive Classroom Discipline
Jacob Kounin	Improving Discipline Through Lesson Management
Marvin Marshall	Discipline Through Raising Responsibility
Fritz Redl and William Wattenberg	Discipline Through Influencing Group Behavior
B. F. Skinner	Discipline Through Shaping Desired Behavior

Other Theorists

Theorist	Approach
Thomas Gordon	Discipline as Self-Control
Barbara Coloroso	Inner Discipline
Linda Albert	Cooperative Discipline
Jane Nelsen, Lynn Lott, and H. Stephen Glenn	Positive Discipline in the Classroom
Alfie Kohn	Beyond Discipline

Lee and Marlene Canter: Assertive Discipline

Lee and Marlene Canter are well-known for Assertive Discipline, their approach to behavior management in the classroom. Their approach is designed to help teachers interact with students in a calm and meaningful manner. The overall goal of their program is to help teachers establish classrooms where they are able to deliver instruction effectively so that the students can learn.

SCENARIO

In Mrs. Snyder's fifth grade class, Sylvia and Jessica have been distracting other students for the past several days. Even after several warnings, they continue to talk during instruction, giggle at inappropriate times, and pass notes throughout the day. Mrs. Snyder has tried several tactics to put a stop to this behavior, but to no avail.

As you read about Lee and Marlene Canter's approach to classroom discipline, consider a variety of strategies to address this situation.

Definition Teachers interact with students in a calm and meaningful way, focusing on positive behavior while providing a climate where students' needs are met.

Goal Students recognize the consequences of their actions, and the teacher's focus shifts from reprimands of negative behavior toward positive praise.

Model
- Students' needs are met.
- Behavior is managed kindly.
- A democratic set of classroom rules is established.
- Appropriate behavior is taught.
- Trust is established.

Outcomes/Expectations
Students
- Students recognize their misbehavior and identify its consequences.
- Students are part of the decision-making process, including rules and consequences.

Teacher
- A classroom free from disruption is established.
- A caring teacher cultivates the best interests and needs of the students.
- Parents and administrators support the Assertive Discipline approach.

Elements

Modeling Teachers model the kind of trust and respect for the students that they want their students to show toward others.

Discipline Plan A discipline plan that is understood and supported by both students and parents is necessary to help students limit their negative behavior.

Positive Statements Teachers repeat directions as positive statements, such as "Victor remembered to raise his hand. Good job." Others will follow.

Positive Support Students enjoy positive support when they behave acceptably. Positive acknowledgment can be very powerful.

Direct Instruction Teachers teach proper class behavior through direct instruction.

Proactive Approach Teachers are most effective when they use a proactive, rather than a reactive, approach to discipline. In a reactive approach, teachers wait until students misbehave and then try to decide what to do to get them back on course. In a proactive approach, teachers anticipate misbehavior and plan in advance how to deal with it in a positive manner.

Actions/Steps

1 · Consider three types of teachers and the effect each has on students.

Hostile teachers

CHARACTERISTICS

- View students as rivals
- Must keep the upper hand in order to maintain discipline
- Are constantly at odds with students

EFFECTS

- Teacher behavior suggests a dislike for students.
- Students may feel they are being treated unfairly.

Nonassertive teachers

CHARACTERISTICS

- Exhibit a passive approach with students
- Don't establish reasonable expectations
- Allow certain behaviors one day but strongly disapprove of them the next day
- Are inconsistent

EFFECT

- Students get confused about expectations.

Assertive teachers

CHARACTERISTICS

- Clearly, confidently, and consistently model and express expectations
- Build trust with the class and help students practice acceptable behavior

EFFECTS
- Students gain a sense of comfort.
- Teaching and learning thrive.

2 · Build trust.
- Establish mutual respect and trust by modeling behavior.
- Listen carefully.
- Speak to students respectfully.
- Treat all students fairly.

3 · Create clear expectations and consequences.
- Establish a discipline hierarchy.
- List corrective actions in the order in which they will be imposed during the day, with each consequence more severe than the preceding consequence.
- Track and record offenses that students commit.
    1 · Color cards: Five colored cards are kept in a pocket chart for each student; a student pulls the designated color card from his or her assigned "pocket" as a particular offense is committed (for the first offense, the student pulls the green card; for the second offense, the student pulls the blue card; and so on).
    2 · Clipboard with student name list: Check marks document offenses.
    3 · Grade book: Check marks document offenses.
    4 · File or journal: Entries document offenses.
NOTE: Don't embarrass students publicly by tracking behavior on the board.

Discipline: Hierarchy of Consequences

First Offense Give the student a verbal warning.

Second Offense Have the student state the rule that was broken and then take a five-minute time-out from recess, free time, computer time, etc.

Third Offense Tell the student that he or she has chosen the consequence of a note/phone call home.

Fourth Offense Tell the student that he or she has chosen to go to another teacher's classroom.

Fifth Offense Tell the student that he or she has chosen to visit the principal's office.

Severe Clause A specific behavior may be so serious (for example, fighting, spitting, or abusing classroom equipment) that it is best to invoke the "severe clause" by sending the student to the principal's office on the first offense.

4 · Redirect nondisruptive behavior.

- Often, students break class rules in a nondisruptive way. Instead of applying corrective actions for these benign misbehaviors, teachers should redirect students' behavior, guiding them back to the assigned task.
- Teachers might consider the following tactics:
  - Use "the look"—Make eye contact and use an expression that shows awareness and disapproval.
  - Use physical proximity—Move close to or beside the student. Usually, there is no need to do more.
  - Mention the offending students' names—"I want all of you, including José and Monique, to come up with three sentences."
  - Use proximity verbal recognition—If Jason is not working, but Alyssa and Mylah, seated nearby, are working, say, "Alyssa and Mylah are doing a good job of completing their work."

SOLUTION

Remember Sylvia and Jessica in Mrs. Snyder's fifth grade class? Now that you have had a quick look at the Canters' system of Assertive Discipline, how might you approach the situation? Be sure to consider the diversity of students (culture, special needs, learning styles, language ability, etc.) when answering this question.

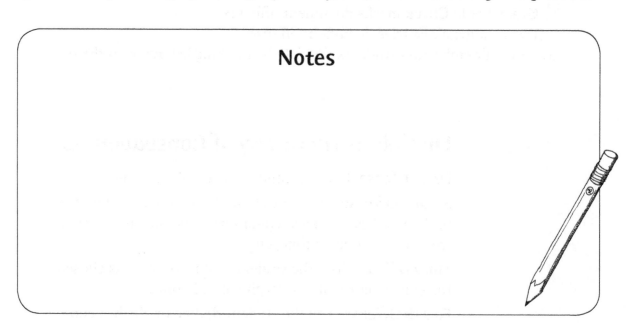

ADDITIONAL READING

Canter, L. *Assertive Discipline: Positive Behavior Management for Today's Classroom.* 2009. Solution Tree. (ISBN 9781934009154)

Canter, L. *Classroom Management for Academic Success.* 2005. Solution Tree. (ISBN 9781932127836)

Canter, L., and M. Canter. *Parents on Your Side: A Teacher's Guide to Creating Positive Relationships with Parents.* 2008. Solution Tree. (ISBN 9781934009192)

Richard Curwin and Allen Mendler: Discipline with Dignity

Richard Curwin and Allen Mendler's central idea is that procedures that establish a sense of dignity and hope provide students with opportunities for success in school. One of the many responsibilities of teachers is to help students believe that school is beneficial and that they can exert control over their own lives. Even though most students behave so as to prevent damage to their dignity, many frequently misbehave and are considered to be behavior problems because of it.

SCENARIO

Mr. Matsura has been struggling with Joseph since the beginning of the school year. Joseph causes routine disruptions, is often aggressive on the playground, and constantly argues with Mr. Matsura, other students, and other adults. He rarely turns in homework, and his classwork is sloppy and usually incomplete. Mr. Matsura has tried to involve the parents, but he has received no support from the home. He finds himself losing his temper in front of other students when responding to Joseph's behavior.

As you read about Richard Curwin and Allen Mendler's approach to classroom discipline, consider a variety of strategies to address this situation.

Definition Students will have success in school if there are procedures in place that establish a sense of dignity and hope.

Goal Students believe that school can be beneficial and that they can exert control over their own lives. A student's dignity is important.

Model

- Discipline is a very important part of teaching.
- Short-term solutions are rarely effective.
- Students must always be treated with dignity.
- Discipline must not interfere with the motivation to learn.
- Responsibility is more important than obedience.
- Responsibility, not obedience, is the goal of discipline.
- Responsibility, which involves making good decisions, almost always produces better long-term behavior than does obedience of teacher demands.

- Consequences (pre-planned results that are invoked when class rules are broken) are necessary in discipline. Consequences are most effective when jointly planned by the teacher and students.
- The behavior of difficult-to-manage students can be improved through interesting lessons on topics of personal relevance that permit active involvement and lead to competencies that students consider important.

Outcomes/Expectations
Students
- Students experience success in school.
- Students have a sense of dignity and hope.
- Students sense a connection to life.

Teacher
- The teacher helps students believe that school can be beneficial.
- The teacher helps students exert control over their own lives.

Elements
Preventing Escalation of Conflicts
- Use active listening.
- Arrange to speak with a student later.
- Keep all communication as private as possible.
- Invoke the insubordination rule, which removes a student from the room if the student refuses to accept a consequence.

Motivating Difficult Students
- Select lesson topics that have personal importance and relevance to the students.
- Set up authentic learning goals, which lead to genuine competence that students can display and be proud of.
- Involve students actively in lessons.
- Give students opportunities to take risks and make decisions without fear of failure.
- Show genuine energy and interest in the topics being studied.
- Every day, do at least one activity that is different.
- Choose class activities that students will look forward to.

Actions/Steps
1 · Be consistent. If a student breaks a rule, it is always best to implement a consequence.
2 · State the rule and its consequence simply and calmly. No scolding is necessary.
3 · Use the power of proximity at a conversational distance, and one step closer.
4 · Make personal and/or eye contact, but maintain this contact for no more than a minute. Keep cultural considerations about direct eye contact in mind.

5 · Use a soft voice. This is much more effective than yelling. Maintain dignity.

6 · Catch the student being good. Try to do this two to three times per hour. Speak softly.

7 · Don't embarrass the student in front of the class. Maintain dignity and avoid power struggles.

8 · Speak firmly but without anger when stating a consequence.

9 · Don't accept excuses, bargaining, or whining.

SOLUTION

Remember Joseph in Mr. Matsura's class? Now that you have had a quick look at Curwin and Mendler's system of Discipline with Dignity, how might you approach the situation? Consider the diversity of students (culture, special needs, learning styles, language ability, etc.) when answering this question.

Notes

ADDITIONAL READING

Curwin, R., A. Mendler, and B. Mendler. *Discipline with Dignity: New Challenges, New Solutions.* 2008. Association for Supervision and Curriculum Development. (ISBN 9781416607465)

Mendler, A. *What Do I Do When . . . ? How to Achieve Discipline with Dignity in the Classroom.* 2007. Solution Tree. (ISBN 9781934009079)

Mendler, A., and R. Curwin. *Discipline with Dignity for Challenging Youth.* 2009. Solution Tree. (ISBN 9781934009253)

Rudolph Dreikurs: Discipline Through Democratic Teaching

Rudolph Dreikurs emphasizes seeking out and dealing with the underlying causes of misbehavior. He suggests that misbehavior is the result of feeling that one does not belong to a group. When this happens, the student acts out because of a need for power, attention, revenge, or avoidance. Dreikurs' overall goal is for students to be able to cooperate without being penalized or rewarded and to feel that they are valuable contributors to the classroom. He focuses on helping students acquire self-discipline based on an understanding of social value.

SCENARIO

Ms. Shrug began the school year with a list of five very powerful rules written with negative undertones. The students had no part in making these rules, nor did they take part in determining potential consequences. The rules she had in place on the first day of school were the following:

- Students will not talk when the teacher or another student is talking.
- Students will not get out of their seats unless given permission to do so by the teacher.
- Students will be penalized for speaking out of turn or using derogatory language.
- Parents will be called if students engage in violent acts in the classroom or on the playground.
- Students will lose privileges if desks are not maintained and organized.

As you read about Rudolph Dreikurs' approach to classroom discipline, consider ideas that might address this situation.

Definition Students acquire self-discipline based on an understanding of social value.

Goal Teachers seek out and deal with underlying causes of misbehavior to help students acquire self-discipline through a connection to social value.

Model

- Rules are formulated jointly by the teacher and students.
- Logical consequences are established for both compliance and violation.

Outcomes/Expectations

Students

- Students participate in deciding how the class functions.
- Students work with one another and the teacher to make the class function.

Teacher

- The teacher guides shared decision making with students.
- The teacher uses a democratic approach to decide how the class functions.

Elements

- The teacher encourages self-control.
- The teacher develops a democratic classroom, where the teacher and students work together to make decisions on how the class will function.
- The classroom should be neither autocratic (where the teacher makes all the decisions) nor permissive (where the students make all the decisions).
- The teacher should be able to identify faulty goals and correct them.

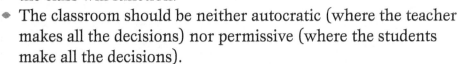
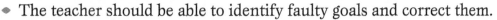

Actions/Steps

1 · Establish a set of rules and consequences.
2 · Enforce the rules consistently.
3 · Adjust the rules and consequences when necessary.
4 · Emphasize social connection.

SOLUTION

Remember Ms. Shrug's classroom rules? Now that you have had a quick look at Rudolph Dreikurs' theory of classroom discipline, how might you develop rules and consequences for your own classroom? Consider the diversity of your students (culture, special needs, learning styles, language ability, etc.) when answering this question.

Notes

ADDITIONAL READING

Dinkmeyer, D., and R. Dreikurs. *Encouraging Children to Learn*. 2000. Routledge. (ISBN 9781583910825)

Dreikurs, R., P. Cassel, and E.D. Ferguson. *Discipline Without Tears: How to Reduce Conflict and Establish Cooperation in the Classroom*. 2004. John Wiley & Sons. (ISBN 9780470835081)

Haim Ginott: Discipline Through Congruent Communication

The Ginott model concentrates on communication between teacher and student. Teachers are encouraged to avoid criticism, try to understand students' feelings, foster student autonomy, and try to help students take responsibility for their actions. These goals are accomplished by establishing communication with the students and by reasoning with them (Edwards, 1993).

SCENARIO

Mr. Sprague has an excellent group of third grade students. They get along well, listen attentively, and participate eagerly. However, there are a few students who struggle to stay on task and often seek negative attention. Mr. Sprague finds himself giving negative feedback from time to time. When one of his students is misbehaving, Mr. Sprague wants to avoid referring to past events and instead focus only on the current situation. His goal is to communicate effectively with his students so he can help them take responsibilities for their actions.

As you read about Haim Ginott's approach to classroom discipline, consider ideas that might apply to Mr. Sprague's desire to help his students behave.

Definition The teacher establishes empathetic communication with students, where he reasons with them without criticizing them.

Goal The teacher establishes communication with students and helps them take responsibility for their actions.

Model
* Communication is established.
* The focus is on behavior, not the person.
* The focus is on the current situation.
* The teacher and student cooperate with each other.

Outcomes/Expectations
Students
* Students are given a fresh start.
* Students actively participate in communication.

Teacher
* The teacher invites students to cooperate.
* The teacher is nonjudgmental.
* The teacher creates a risk-free environment, where students are comfortable voicing their opinions and needs.

Elements
* Teachers use harmonious communication that focuses on students' feelings about situations and themselves.
* The cardinal principle of congruent communication is that it addresses situations, not a student's character or personality.

* Learning always takes place in the present tense; students are not prejudged.
* Learning is always a personal matter to a student; each child is an individual.
* Teachers do not preach, moralize, impose guilt, or demand promises.
* Teachers do not label students, belittle them, or denigrate their character.
* An effective teacher invites cooperation from his or her students.
* The teacher asks, "How can I be more helpful to my students?"
* Teachers respect each student's privacy.
* When correcting students, the teacher provides directions for the desired behavior.
* The teacher avoids asking "why" questions when discussing behavior.
* Sarcasm is almost always dangerous and is not used when discussing a situation.

Actions/Steps
1 · Don't prejudge students.
2 · Focus on the behavior, not on the student.
3 · Encourage participation from students.

SOLUTION

Remember Mr. Sprague? Now that you have had a quick look at the theory of Haim Ginott, how might you approach communicating effectively with your own students? Consider the diversity of your students (culture, special needs, learning styles, language ability, etc.) when answering this question.

Notes

ADDITIONAL READING

Ginott, H. *Between Parent and Child.* 1976. Harper Collins Publishers. (ISBN 9780380008216)

Ginott, H. *Between Parent and Teenager.* 1982. HarperCollins Publishers. (ISBN 9780380008209)

Ginott, H. *Teacher and Child: A Book for Parents and Teachers.* 1993. Simon & Schuster Adult Publishing Group. (ISBN 9780020139744)

William Glasser: Noncoercive Discipline

William Glasser believes that improvement in education and discipline can only be accomplished by changing the way classrooms function. He says that it is clear that trying to force students to learn or behave properly will not succeed. He focuses on providing a curriculum that is attractive to students and on working with them in ways that encourage them to make responsible choices that lead to personal success.

It is the responsibility of the teacher to teach students that they are the ones who choose how they act. "The teacher's task is to help students make good choices by making clear the connection between student behavior and its consequences" (Emmer, 1986, p. 7). According to Glasser (1989), pushing a student into a corner until he or she conforms to the teacher's expectations is not in accordance with a psychologically healthy adolescent.

SCENARIO

Mrs. Currie teaches fourth grade. Her district requires that she use a mandated curriculum that is systematic in its approach but doesn't always take into account the "whole child" or the interests and cultural backgrounds of the students. She notices that some of the students in her class roll their eyes, make negative comments about being bored, and don't eagerly participate no matter how positive she is or how many strategies she employs.

As you read about William Glasser's approach to teaching and ways to avoid misbehavior, consider ideas that might address her desire to make the curriculum more attractive to her students.

Definition Motivated by a stimulating curriculum, students make responsible choices that lead to their personal success.

Goal The teacher guides students to make their own responsible choices that lead to their personal success.

Model
- The teacher helps students make good choices.
- The teacher connects student behavior to consequences.
- The teacher provides an attractive curriculum to motivate students.

Outcomes/Expectations
Students
- Students participate in how the class functions.

Teacher
- The teacher guides shared decision making with students.

Elements
- Basic student needs are met (survival, belonging, power, freedom, and fun).
- Students connect to the curriculum and find it meaningful.
- Students have input into class rules and consequences.
- Students have opportunities to discuss their misbehavior.

Actions/Steps
1 · Develop a quality curriculum that includes discussion opportunities, exploration, and depth, and that is attractive to the students.
2 · Decide if you will be a "lead" teacher (one who cultivates learning in a student-centered approach) or a "boss" teacher (one who imposes requirements without student input).
3 · Provide a warm and supportive classroom environment.

SOLUTION

Remember Mrs. Currie? Now that you have had a quick look at William Glasser's method, how might you approach planning an engaging curriculum for your own students? Consider the diversity of your students (culture, special needs, learning styles, language ability, etc.) when answering this question.

Notes

ADDITIONAL READING

Glasser, W. *Choice Theory in the Classroom.* HarperPerennial. 1998. (ISBN 9780060952877)

Glasser, W. *The Quality School: Managing Students Without Coercion.* 1998. HarperPerennial. (ISBN 9780060952860)

Glasser, W. *The Quality School Teacher: A Companion Volume to The Quality School.* 1998. HarperPerennial. (ISBN 9780060952853)

Fred Jones: Positive Classroom Discipline

Fred Jones has developed a model of classroom discipline that accentuates the physical presence of the teacher. Interrupting instruction, staring, and sitting and standing close to students are powerful techniques that should stop students from misbehaving (Edwards, 1993). Jones is the first theorist to place major emphasis on nonverbal communication, such as a teacher's body language, facial expressions, gestures, eye contact, and physical proximity. He emphasizes the value of good classroom organization and management and stresses the importance of teaching students to behave responsibly. Jones primarily focuses on helping students support their own self-control so that they behave properly and maintain a positive attitude.

Jones notes that about 95 percent of student misbehavior consists of talking to neighbors and being out of one's seat, as well as general goofing off, such as daydreaming and making noise. Teachers in typical classrooms lose, on average, about 50 percent of their teaching time because students are off task or otherwise disrupting learning. Most teaching time now lost in this way can be recouped if teachers establish clear classroom structures, use effective body language, use "Say, See, Do" teaching, use incentive systems, and provide efficient help to students.

SCENARIO

Mr. Alfaretta, who has been teaching for over two decades, is teaching second grade this year. He maintains strong classroom organization, employs good management skills, and stresses the importance of teaching students to behave responsibly. While these are all important components of classroom management, they carry over into his delivery of instruction and often produce a sense of fear in the students. The students have been complaining that he only lectures and rarely includes them in the learning process.

As you read about Fred Jones' approach to classroom discipline, consider strategies that would include students in the learning process and ways to develop alternatives to managing discipline.

Definition The teacher establishes clear classroom structures, uses effective body language, uses "Say, See, Do" teaching, uses incentive systems, and provides efficient help to students.

Goal The teacher uses classroom structure, body language, and an organized incentive program, while actively involving students to elicit responsibility and good behavior.

Model

Structuring the Classroom to Discourage Misbehavior

Room arrangement Minimize the physical distance between teacher and students. This allows the teacher to "work the crowd."

Classroom chores Assign as many classroom chores to students as possible. This gives students a sense of buy-in to the class program.

Opening routines Begin the class with bell work, which does not require active instruction from the teacher. Bell work engages and focuses students on the day's lesson, and they can begin on their own as soon as they are seated at their desks.

Using Effective Body Language

Proper breathing Remain calm in every situation.

Eye contact Turn and point your feet and eyes toward talking students. This shows a teacher's commitment to discipline.

Body carriage Hold yourself erect and move assertively, even when you are tired or troubled.

Facial expressions Use facial expressions to communicate with the students.

Using "Say, See, Do" Teaching

Many teachers spend a large portion of a class period presenting information to students while the students remain passive, and then, at the end of the lesson, ask the students to do something:

> TEACHER *Input · Input · Input · Input · Input · · ·* STUDENT *Output*

The most effective teacher puts students to work from the very beginning, presenting information and then quickly having students do something with it:

> TEACHER *Input · · ·* STUDENT *Input · · ·* TEACHER *Input · · ·* STUDENT *Input · · ·*
> TEACHER *Input · · ·* STUDENT *Output*

This approach is "Say, See, Do" teaching. The teacher *says* (or *does*), the students *see,* and the students *do* something with the input.

Training Responsibility Through Incentive Systems

An incentive is an external device or tactic that prompts an individual to act in a certain way. It is promised as a consequence for desired behavior, but is deferred. It could be more time in the computer lab, a preferred activity, or an unspecified surprise.

Outcomes/Expectations

Students

- Students behave responsibly.
- Students are actively involved in learning.
- Students receive incentives.

Teacher

The teacher uses body language to communicate.
- The teacher uses "Say, See, Do" teaching.

Elements

- Efficient arrangement of the classroom permits the teacher to work the crowd as he or she supervises student work and provides help.
- Proper use of body language is one of the most effective discipline skills available to teachers. Eye contact, physical proximity, body carriage, facial expressions, and gestures are all part of body language.
- "Say, See, Do" teaching is an instructional method that calls for frequent student response to teacher input. It keeps students alert and actively involved in the lesson.
- Students will work hard and behave well when given incentives to do so. To be effective, an incentive must be attractive to the entire class and be equally available to all students.

Actions/Steps

1 · Be aware of your body language at all times.
2 · Incorporate "Say, See, Do" teaching in planning and instruction.
3 · Actively involve learners.
4 · Include incentives.

SOLUTION

Remember Mr. Alfaretta? Now that you have had a quick look at Fred Jones' theory of classroom discipline, how might you approach the delivery of instruction and alternative discipline strategies? Consider the diversity of students (culture, special needs, learning styles, language ability, etc.) when answering this question.

Notes

ADDITIONAL READING

Jones, F., P. Jones, and J.L. Jones. *Fred Jones Tools for Teaching: Discipline, Instruction, Motivation* [with DVD]. 2007. Fredric H. Jones & Associates, Inc. (ISBN 9780965026321)

Jacob Kounin: Improving Discipline Through Lesson Management

Jacob Kounin focuses on how classroom management and instructional management affect student behavior in school. He focuses on the importance of giving detailed instructions, as well as on how lessons are planned, organized, and executed, in order to maintain appropriate student behavior and keep students engaged. Kounin spotlights how a ripple effect comes about, when one student's misbehavior spreads to others. He believes that by implementing fluidity in lesson delivery, misbehaviors can be minimized.

SCENARIO

Ms. Beck has been having difficulty with her sixth grade students during cooperative group work. The students are assigned to specific groups so that they know where to go and with whom they will be working, but she is struggling with the rotation transitions as students prepare to move from one group to the next. During instruction, Ms. Beck has no problem with smooth transitions and uses a variety of strategies (such as a bell, a five-finger countdown, and a patterned clap) that signal students to finish one task before starting the next one. When it comes to group transitions, however, she is not as smooth in getting students to rotate from one task to the next.

As you read about Jacob Kounin's approach to classroom discipline, consider the various strategies Ms. Beck could use to make her students' group transitions more fluid.

Definition Instructional management directly affects student behavior. If a teacher plans and paces lessons well and is always prepared with the materials, he or she will have success delivering instruction and maintaining smooth transitions.

Goal An organized instructional system of management is created, one that supports positive student behavior and fluid transitions with an awareness of what is going on in the classroom at all times.

Model

- The teacher is aware of what is happening in all parts of the classroom.
- The classroom and its management are well organized.
- Lessons are strategically paced and managed.
- Students are continuously engaged.
- Students are aware of their role as part of the whole group.

Outcomes/Expectations

Students

- Students perceive that the teacher knows what is happening at all times—"She has eyes in the back of her head."
- Students always have something to do.
- Students recognize that they are part of the larger group.
- Students can reflect on the productivity of their actions and change their behavior accordingly.
- Students never have to guess what is expected of them.

Teacher

- The teacher communicates expectations and considers possible behavior so that he or she is "with it" at all times.
- The teacher halts misbehavior before it has a chance to "ripple" to other students.
- The teacher has organizational systems in place for everything—from where to submit classroom work to "May Do" options for early finishers.
- The teacher holds students responsible for their actions.
- The teacher encourages student motivation, attention, and participation.
- The teacher maintains a high sense of energy and enthusiasm.

Elements

- **"With-it"-ness** (the teacher's ability to know what is going on in his or her classroom at all times)—The key is that students perceive that the teacher knows what is happening at all times. The teacher knows his or her students on a personal level—by name, interests, and ability, for example.

- **Overlapping** (multitasking, presenting the lesson while preventing inappropriate behavior)—This means that the teacher is prepared for all scenarios. For example, the teacher has materials ready for students who finish classroom work early, and students who arrive late know exactly where to find what they need and what procedures to follow. All the while, the teacher continues the lesson.
- **Momentum** (the flow of the lesson, knowing when to slow down and when to move on)—This involves having a clear objective and keeping the lesson succinct and to the point so that students stay engaged. To keep students moving, a timer may be helpful. Momentum also involves flexibility and going with the flow. When a lesson is interrupted—there is a technology malfunction, for example—the teacher adapts immediately and makes the necessary adjustments to move forward with the lesson.
- **Smoothness** (keeping everything moving despite outside distractions, such as unrelated questions, students leaving early, and all-call announcements)— The teacher is able to stay on topic and stick to the lesson plan. Smoothness also involves circulating to facilitate students' cooperation and discussion as they work in small groups.
- **Group focus** (engagement of the whole class)—This challenging element includes meeting the needs of a diverse learning community. The teacher holds the class's attention, moving around the room, asking questions, checking for understanding, and encouraging students.
- Whether as a class or in small groups, students are accountable as contributing members of a group and will be graded as such.

Actions/Steps

1 · Create an organized classroom, where students have a place for everything.
2 · Make sure that students understand classroom procedures.
3 · Know your students, and be aware of everything that is happening at all times.
4 · Be engaged and enthusiastic.
5 · Plan and pace your lessons well.
6 · Establish clear expectations.
7 · Address inappropriate behavior to avoid the "ripple effect."
8 · Stress the importance of positive behavior, student motivation, and class participation.

SOLUTION

Remember Ms. Beck? Now that you have had a quick look at the theory of Jacob Kounin, how might you approach the delivery of instruction and keep your lessons flowing? Consider the diversity of your students (culture, special needs, learning styles, language ability, etc.) when answering this question.

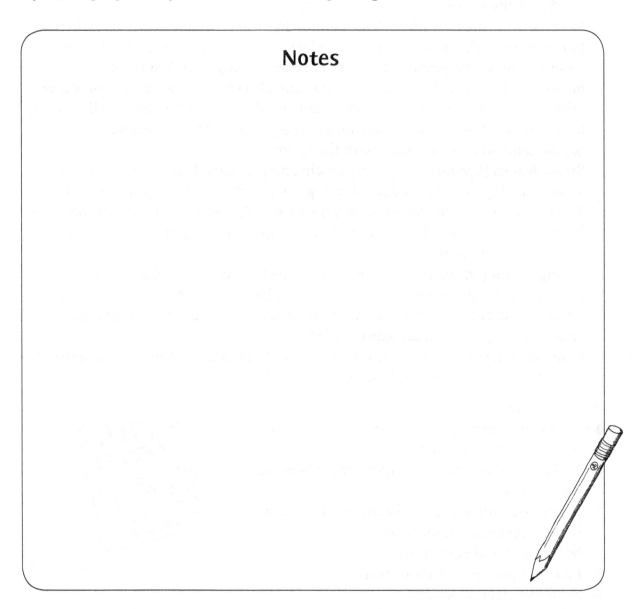

Notes

ADDITIONAL READING

Charles, C.M. *Building Classroom Discipline.* 2010. Prentice Hall. (ISBN 9780137034055)

Kounin, J.S. *Discipline and Group Management in Classrooms.* 1977. Krieger Publishing Company. (ISBN 9780882755045)

Wolfgang, C.H. *Solving Discipline and Classroom Management Problems: Methods and Models for Today's Teachers,* ed. 7. 2008. John Wiley and Sons. (ISBN 9780470129104)

Marvin Marshall: Discipline Through Raising Responsibility

Marvin Marshall's focus is helping students conduct themselves in a socially and personally responsible manner, leading to desirable classroom behavior for students at all levels. He also shows how parents can use this approach to build responsibility in their children and suggests that all of us can benefit from adopting and using three principles in our daily lives: positivity, choice, and reflection. "Responsibility finds a way; irresponsibility finds an excuse" is Marshall's claim.

SCENARIO

Ms. Fischer's first graders love to answer questions, go out of their way to help one another, and offer to assist the teacher in keeping the classroom clean and organized. In any situation, this would be ideal. However, the reason most of the students in the class do these things is because they are rewarded each time with treats, such as candy, cookies, and pretzels, or with stickers, hand stamps, or free time—extrinsic rewards for helping. Unfortunately, when Ms. Fischer asks her students to do something, they ask what they will get in return.

As you read about Marvin Marshall's approach to classroom management and discipline, consider a variety of strategies to encourage student participation.

Definition Students benefit from adopting and using three principles in their daily lives: positivity, choice, and reflection.

Goal Students demonstrate more responsible classroom behavior without the use of extrinsic rewards.

Model
- Teachers use noncoercive tactics.
- Levels of the behavior hierarchy are delineated.
- Students reflect on their behavior.
- Students conduct themselves responsibly.

Outcomes/Expectations
Students
* Students accept responsibility.
* Students conduct themselves responsibly.
* Students adopt and use the three principles in their daily lives.

Teacher
* The teacher uses a noncoercive approach to discipline.
* The teacher uses a hierarchy of social behavior.
* Character education is taught.
* The teacher checks for understanding.
* The teacher redirects inappropriate behavior.

Elements
* As students show more personal responsibility, classroom behavior improves.

* In order to achieve improvement, external incentives for student behavior are abandoned; the teacher stops using rewards for appropriate behavior, using punishments for inappropriate behavior, telling students what to do, warning them, and criticizing them.
* Noncoercive influence tactics replace coercion. A major noncoercive tactic involves posing questions that prompt students to reflect on their behavior.
* A hierarchy of social behavior is used to facilitate the reflective process:

Level A   Anarchy
Level B   Bothering/Bossing/Bullying
Level C   Cooperating/Conforming
Level D   Taking the initiative to be responsible.

When students function at Level D, they make enlightened decisions about personal behavior. Their decisions result in responsible conduct, regardless of circumstances, personal urges, and the influence of others.
* When students reflect on their inappropriate behavior, they immediately see how they could behave better.
* Undesirable behavior is considered separately from students as persons.

Actions/Steps

1 · Develop responsible behavior.

Marshall contends that the best way to help students conduct themselves properly is to encourage them to accept personal responsibility for their behavior.

The responsibility approach has the following benefits:

- It reduces discipline problems, referrals, class removals, and suspensions.
- It handles classroom disruption simply and easily.
- It uses authority without resorting to punishment.
- It increases individual and social responsibility.
- It reduces the influence of peer pressure.
- It integrates character education.
- It promotes learning.
- It reduces stress.

Marshall urges teachers to rely on internal motivation and to stop trying to motivate students externally, as many teachers do today.

2 · Encourage internal motivation in students.

This approach has the following benefits:

- It emphasizes the power of choice.
- It encourages students to think and to ask reflective questions.
- It creates curiosity and desire in students.
- It emphasizes a sense of personal responsibility.
- It uses acknowledgment and recognition.
- It makes use of collaboration.
- It generates excitement in the teacher.
- It uses variety.

3 · Heighten positive thinking in school through reflection and self-evaluation while establishing good relationships.

This approach has the following benefits:

- It changes negative statements into positive ones.
- Students think and speak positively.
- It fosters interpersonal relations.
- Students see situations as challenges, not problems.
- Relationships are improved through classroom meetings.

SOLUTION

Remember Ms. Fischer? Now that you have had a quick look at Marvin Marshall's theory, how might you approach motivating your students intrinsically? Consider the diversity of your students (culture, special needs, learning styles, language ability, etc.) when answering this question.

Notes

ADDITIONAL READING

Marshall, M. *Discipline Without Stress, Punishments, or Rewards: How Teachers and Parents Promote Responsibility & Learning.* 2001. Piper Press. (ISBN 9780970060617)

Fritz Redl and William Wattenberg: Discipline Through Influencing Group Behavior

Fritz Redl and William Wattenberg propose that teachers support a student's own self-control mechanisms. Since individual behaviors differ from behaviors within a group, classroom discipline must be achieved by influencing group behavior. They also believe in the pleasure-pain principle, by which the teacher provides opportunities to produce a range of pleasant to unpleasant experiences. This is meant to elicit good feelings about a pleasant experience in order to motivate students to repeat a desirable behavior, while bad feelings about an unpleasant experience will lead to avoidance of the undesirable behavior (Redl and Wattenberg, 1959).

SCENARIO

Mrs. Williams includes the use of cooperative learning groups in her lesson planning. For the most part, students enjoy working together in these groups, but she notices that there is sometimes a lot of unnecessary chatter and copying of one another's work. Mrs. Williams wants to continue including groups in her planning, but she isn't sure how to make this type of learning meaningful and productive.

As you read about Fritz Redl and William Wattenberg's approach to classroom management and discipline, consider ways in which Mrs. Williams can organize groups so that work gets accomplished and students learn from one another.

Definition Students behave differently in groups, and teachers can influence students to control classroom behavior.

Goal Student behavior is managed through influencing behavior in a group setting.

Model

- Teachers influence students.
- Group behavior affects individual behavior.
- Students are involved in establishing rules and consequences.

- Punishment is avoided, and self-control is supported.
- The connection between conduct and consequences is demonstrated (Bucher and Manning, 2001/2002).

Outcomes/Expectations

Students

- Students learn self-control.
- Students relate to the group.

Teacher

- The teacher influences and supports self-control.
- The teacher consistently shows the relationship between behavior and consequences.

Elements

- People in groups behave differently than they do individually.
- Group dynamics strongly affect behavior.
- Students adopt identifiable roles in the classroom (for example, as leaders, followers, instigators, and scapegoats).
- The teacher is cast into many different roles that affect student behavior (for example, as a role model).
- The teacher involves students in setting class standards (rules) and deciding how transgressions are handled (consequences).
- Teachers use influence techniques rather than punishment to control behavior (for example, they support self-control, appraisal, and so on).
- Punishment is a last resort in dealing with misbehavior.

Actions/Steps

1 · Establish opportunities for group work.
2 · Offer chances for students to take leadership roles.
3 · Plan for student role-play of actions for self-control.
4 · Include occasions for the pleasure-pain principle to be applied.
5 · Hold discussions about behavior and outcomes.

SOLUTION

Remember Mrs. Williams? Now that you have had a quick look at the theory of Fritz Redl and William Wattenberg, how might you approach planning for productive learning groups? Consider the diversity of students (culture, special needs, learning styles, language ability, etc.) when answering this question.

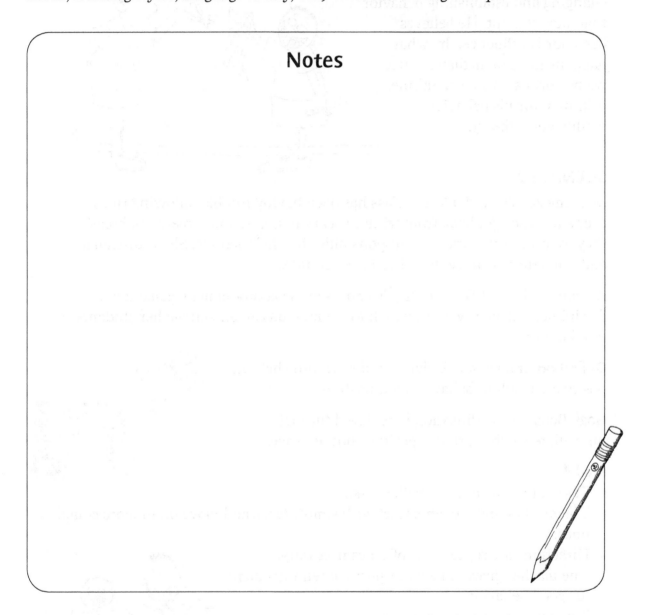

Notes

ADDITIONAL READING

Redl, F. *When We Deal with Children: Selected Writings.* 1972. The Free Press. (ISBN 9780029258804)

B. F. Skinner: Discipline Through Shaping Desired Behavior

B. F. Skinner emphasizes that positive reinforcement is more effective at changing and establishing behavior than punishment. He believes behavior is influenced by what happens to us immediately after we perform a given act. Skinner is known for his behavior modification theory.

SCENARIO

Ms. Amezcua's kindergarten class has been having trouble following rules ever since they got back from winter vacation. Before the three-week break, they followed rules and took responsibility for their actions. She is distraught and not sure how to get her class back on track.

As you read about B. F. Skinner's approach to classroom management and discipline, consider ways in which Ms. Amezcua can encourage her students to follow rules.

Definition Immediate feedback and rewarding behavior positively result in behavior modification.

Goal Behavior modification is achieved through immediate feedback that is positive, not negative.

Model
- Tasks are broken into smaller tasks.
- The teacher and students start with simple tasks and move on to more complex ones.
- Directions are repeated as often as necessary.
- The teacher gives immediate, positive reinforcement for good behavior.
- Tangible incentives may be used.

Outcomes/Expectations
Students
- Students exhibit good behavior through continual reinforcement.

Teacher
- The teacher exhibits consistent reinforcement of behavior.
- The teacher moves from simple to complex tasks.

Elements

- Much, if not most, of our voluntary behavior is shaped by receiving reinforcement immediately after we perform an act.
- If stimuli, or tangible incentives, are to have a reinforcing effect on behavior, they must be received soon after the behavior occurs.
- Behavior modification refers to the overall method of shaping student behavior intentionally through reinforcement.
- Constant reinforcement given at every instance of desirable behavior helps establish new learning.
- Intermittent reinforcement given occasionally is sufficient to maintain desired behavior once it has been established.
- Behaviors that are not reinforced eventually disappear or become extinguished.
- Successive approximation is a behavior-shaping progression in which behavior gets closer to a preset goal.
- Since punishment often has negative effects in behavior modification, it should not be used in the classroom.

Actions/Steps

1 · Use positive rewards, such as a special privilege or extra free time.
2 · Discipline by removing a positive reward, such as loss of a special privilege. Avoid using negative discipline, such as giving extra work.
3 · Give immediate feedback.
4 · Break information into small chunks.

SOLUTION

Remember Ms. Amezcua? Now that you have had a quick look at the theories of B. F. Skinner, how might you approach discipline for your students? Consider the diversity of students (culture, special needs, learning styles, language ability, etc.) when answering this question.

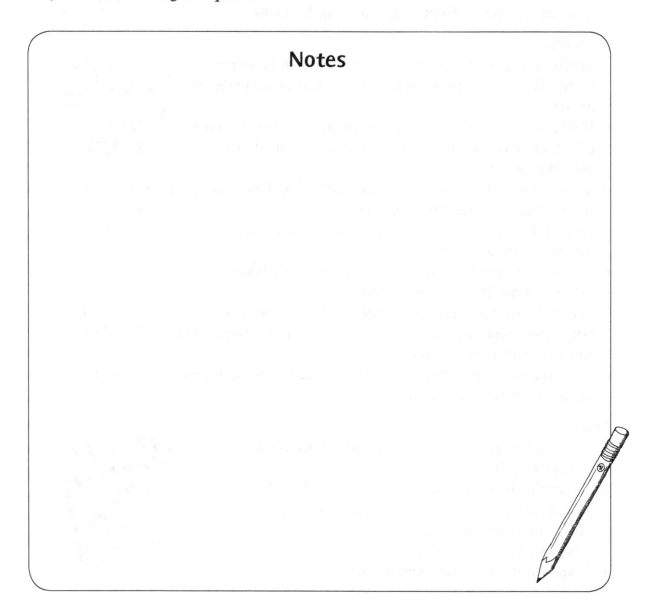

Notes

ADDITIONAL READING

Skinner, B.F. *About Behaviorism*. 1974. Knopf Doubleday Publishing Group. (ISBN 9780394716183)

Skinner, B.F. *Beyond Freedom & Dignity*. 2002 [reprint of 1971 book]. Hackett Publishing Co. (ISBN 9780872206274)

References

Bucher, K., and M. Manning. "Exploring the foundations of middle school classroom management." *Childhood Education*, 78(2), 84–90 (Winter 2001/2002).

Canter, L. "Assertive discipline and the search for the perfect classroom." *Young Children*, 43(2), 24 (January 1988).

Curwin, R., and A. Mendler. *Discipline with Dignity*. Upper Saddle River, N.J.: Prentice-Hall, Inc., 1999.

Edwards, C. *Classroom Discipline and Management*. New York: Macmillan College Division, 1993.

Edwards, C. "Making choices about discipline." *American Secondary Education*, 22(2), 17–21 (1993).

Emmer, E.T. "Effects of teacher training in disciplinary approaches." Washington, D.C.: U.S. Department of Education, Office of Educational Research and Improvement (1986) (ERIC Document Reproduction Service No. ED 316 927).

Glasser, W. *Control Theory in the Practice of Reality Therapy: Case Studies*. New York: HarperPerennial, 1989.

Redl, F., and W.W. Wattenberg. *Mental Hygiene in Teaching*. New York: Harcourt Brace, 1959.

Render, G., J. Padilla, and H. Krank. "What research really shows about assertive discipline." *Educational Leadership*, 46(6), 72–75 (March 1989).

2 Organizing Your Classroom

In an efficient classroom, both teacher and students are able to move easily from one area to another. Learning materials and supplies are easily accessible. Think about classrooms that you have visited where efficiency and smooth transitions were obvious. You will want to model your own classroom organization after these. This chapter introduces key elements to help you set up and organize your classroom so that it is efficient and facilitates learning.

Now that you have your own classroom, consider the following questions:

- What do you do with it?
- How do you set it up?
- Where do the desks go?
- Should you have a desk for the aide or volunteers?
- Where do your supplies go?
- Do you need a rug area?
- Do you need a teacher's desk?
- Will you organize learning centers?
- Should you set up small group stations?

The answers to these questions play a huge role in managing your classroom's physical environment. It is easiest if you start with the big picture and work down to the finer details. With this in mind, start with the physical environment and prioritize the essentials of running a classroom to make sure you're ready on the first day of school.

Physical Arrangement

The physical setting of the classroom is the essential starting point for classroom management. The setting plays a major role in the following areas:

- Classroom efficiency
- Classroom organization
- Teacher and student perceptions of school
- Student behavior
- Student learning
- Student success

It's much easier to plan other aspects of classroom management once you have a clear concept of how the physical features of the classroom will be organized. Here is a practical approach to classroom organization:

1 · Organize the large items: desks, centers, bookcases, file cabinets, tables, and rugs. It is important to consider where your students will sit during read-aloud time, whole group instruction, and collaborative learning, and how they will gather in your classroom library, learning centers, and other areas. Once the large items are placed, you will be able to visualize your classroom experience.

2 · Tackle the bulletin boards. Select a good color that you can live with for the background; use complementary borders. Plan the items that will go on each board and locate the boards strategically. Announcements and calendars can be placed in central locations; subject boards can be placed near corresponding centers. Once your bulletin boards are up and your large items are arranged, you have a motivating environment that carries your signature and invites you to continue the process.

3 · Organize your supplies and closets. Having a place for everything and putting everything in its place will help your classroom run smoothly. During this process, keep in mind the different types of storage containers, such as boxes and baskets. (What will scissors go in? Extra crayons?) Also think about what your students will keep at their desks. What materials do you want them to have readily available? What materials would be too much of a distraction?

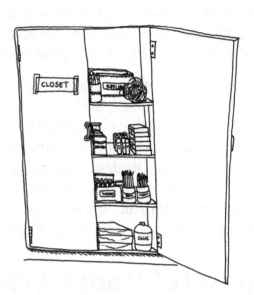

4 · Place and organize materials and books. Start with your desk and the materials and supplies that you will be using. Visualize your school day and where supplies need to be in order to facilitate access and instruction. Place your library books, student books, teacher resource books, and teacher's editions where they will be most easily accessible. Designate bookshelves for specific curricular areas. Place equipment close to where it will be used (for example, projectors near screens). Make sure electrical equipment is near an electrical outlet.

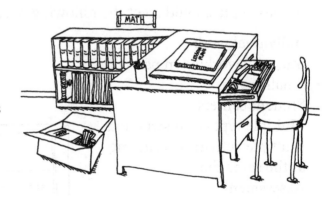

Once all this is in place, your classroom is basically set up! Now you can focus on the details—everything from markers for your dry-erase board to office referrals in your desk. Mentally walk through your day. Will you have what you need when you take attendance, write on the board, or present a lesson? Get as close as you can to being ready. You will never have everything you need, but being as prepared as possible will make things easier when you don't.

Once desks are arranged, other furniture is in place, bookcases and storage have a place, and electronic equipment is up and running, then you can consider developing lesson plans, discipline plans, and other aspects of classroom management without being distracted by the bigger picture of physically setting up the classroom.

Teachers must remember that classroom management is not just a matter of dealing with behavior issues, but of making sure that the environment and atmosphere support the following objectives:

- Student involvement and engagement
- Self-control and self-discipline
- Prevention of disruptions resulting from a disorganized classroom
- A space that shows students they are cared for and respected
- A place where every student, regardless of background or ability, feels included
- A space that signals that every student is held to high expectations
- Maneuverability for students with special physical needs (who use a wheelchair or walker, for example, or who need more space for movement)

Purposeful Room Arrangement

Teachers and students spend most of their waking hours together in the classroom. The classroom should be arranged in a way that takes into account the needs of all persons involved.

Your classroom should meet the following needs:

- Individual work
- Students working in pairs
- Small groups
- Student centers
- Multiple types of instruction
- Multiple activities occurring at the same time
- Assessment
- Monitoring students
- Emergency evacuations
- Special needs of students

Inheriting a Classroom

If you are taking over a classroom that has been left unkempt, is full of old teaching materials, and/or is stocked with textbooks published 20 years ago, it's best to start in one section of the room and work your way around the room.

- Get a large recycling bin and trash can before you begin.
- Start in one corner.
- Don't spend too much time going through materials; quickly assess the items left behind.
- Organize materials you decide to keep and store them by subject area.
- Keep items that directly pertain to your curriculum, aren't dated, and that you connect with.
- If the materials left behind don't look like they have been touched in years, recycle or discard them. This may include the following items:
  - Faded poster paper
  - Butcher paper
  - Construction paper
  - Glue or paste that has hardened
  - Crayons that aren't usable
  - Ink pens that have dried out
  - Chalk that can't be used on the white board
  - Children's books with no front or back cover or that are missing several pages

  - Teaching worksheets unrelated to your grade level or to current standards
  - Resource or activity books that are outdated
  - Files of outdated art activities requiring supplies that are no longer available
- Keep any remaining items for one year; if you haven't used them after a year, recycle or discard them.
- Keep in mind that you need clean, organized space for your own materials and supplies.

Once you have cleared the classroom of unnecessary materials, you will have more space to arrange furniture and organize your wall space.

High-Traffic Areas

Classrooms take on a life of their own, and anticipating potential problem areas reduces the likelihood of classroom disruptions. Certain areas in a classroom may invite misbehavior if they are not carefully planned, organized, and monitored:

- Learning centers
- Classroom library
- Rug area
- Sink area
- Coatracks
- Trash cans
- Drinking fountain
- Pencil sharpener
- Teacher's desk

Planning for space between these areas will help prevent students from congregating in one place for too long a time, which would allow them to distract or interfere with nearby students. Students need to be able to get from one place to another easily without bumping into other students. This takes planning on your part. Physically walk around the classroom as if you were a student, and consider the following questions:

- Is there enough space for me to move through a given area?
- What is my proximity to other students when in a given area?
- What is my proximity to materials or supplies when in this area? Could they become a distraction?
- How visible am I to the teacher?

In this way, you can be proactive in the design of your classroom. Once students are present and interacting, you can modify and adjust the setup and organization as needed during the school year, but this will get you off to a good start.

Also consider the classroom setup from the point of view of the teacher. Physically walk around the classroom, and consider the following questions:

- Is there enough space to circulate around the room easily?
- Can I easily check on groups and individuals?
- Can I see the entire class from several vantage points?
- Are materials easily accessible?
- Can we easily evacuate the room if necessary?

Last, having more than one pencil sharpener and trash can reduces the need for students to conduct such business in clusters, allowing these tasks to be completed more quickly and in a more orderly fashion.

Student Accessibility to Teacher and Instruction

Even though the teacher has access to students when circulating around the room, he or she cannot tend to all the students all of the time. Accessibility is crucial to efficient classroom management and instruction.

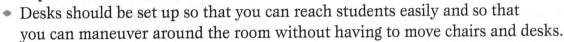

- Students must be able to be easily seen even if you are not right next to them. This is imperative.
- Desks should be set up so that you can reach students easily and so that you can maneuver around the room without having to move chairs and desks.
- Each center and small group table should have enough chairs.
- All materials and supplies need to be accessible to students.
- Learning charts, such as alphabet cards and 100s charts, should be visible to all students.

Walk through every area of the classroom one more time, looking for spots where students can hide or otherwise be where you cannot see them.

Teacher and Student Supply Kits

In order to avoid disrupting a lesson in order to find a dry-erase marker, a pencil, or chart paper, you may want to consider using readily available teacher or student supply kits. Each time you or your students have to interrupt a lesson to look for supplies, you risk losing the attention of several of the students. Whenever this happens, you lose momentum in the delivery of your lesson and it requires time to get students refocused.

Teacher Kit

Find a container to hold your materials and supplies so that they are easily available—perhaps a lightweight tool box or fishing tackle box (with its many compartments), a cleaning caddy with a handle, or a plastic set of drawers on wheels.

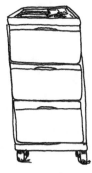

Can you move it around the room? Does it offer you the space and organizational setup you need? Think about a typical day and decide what materials and supplies you frequently use both when planning and delivering instruction. The following items may be included:

- Pencils (for teacher use and extras for students)
- Pens
- Markers
- Colored pencils
- Dry-erase markers
- Sharpies
- Paper
- Post-it Notes
- Scissors
- Stickers
- Stamps and ink pad
- Stapler and staples
- Paper clips
- Student rewards and certificates
- Dictionary and thesaurus

Student Kits

Student kits containing supplies that students frequently use can be placed in or on student desks. It is important to consider managing these supplies in a way that minimizes distraction. Is it better to pass out supplies when needed, or will students be trained to access supplies only as needed? Consider whether each student will have his or her own kit or will share a kit with others. Make sure that student kits work for your management style and classroom routine.

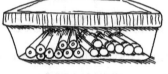

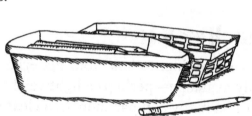

Find containers for student kits that look neat and can stay organized. Consider plastic pencil boxes with lids, small cardboard boxes assembled with brads (possibly available at your school), plastic baskets or tubs, and even plastic zipper bags.

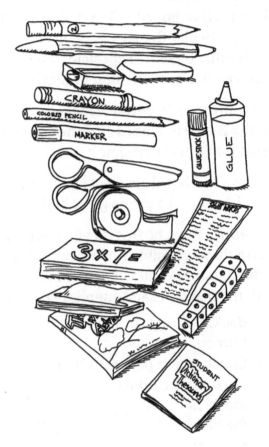

Decide if student kits should contain only supplies or if learning aids (for example, flash cards, readers, and word lists) should be included, too. Will they include art supplies such as glue and scissors? Should there be anything in the kit that could be a distraction? The following items could be included in student kits:

- Pencils
- Pens (for correcting or editing)
- Crayons
- Colored pencils
- Markers*
- Erasers
- Pencil sharpeners*
- Scissors*
- Glue sticks*
- Glue*
- Tape*
- Flash cards
- Word lists (for example, of sight words and vocabulary)
- Kleenex
- Small story books
- Dictionary and thesaurus
- Math manipulatives

---

*These items may cause distraction or are messy; you may want to distribute them on an as-needed basis.

47

Bulletin Boards

Bulletin boards display student work and the teacher's organization. They give an important first impression of what type of learning is going on in the classroom and how that learning is managed. Good bulletin boards can set the stage for a welcoming classroom. Great ideas for bulletin boards include the following:

- **Class News board**—Agendas, schedules, newsletters, and bulletins
- **Procedures board**—Teacher or room list, classroom routines, groups, emergency information, and inclement weather procedures
- **Curricular boards**—Writing, Math, Arts, Science, Social Studies, Health, Holidays, and so forth. The **Bulletin Board Labels** template can be used for this purpose.
- **Interactive board**—Post-it Note comments, questions, and pictures related to a particular theme
- **Calendar board**—Especially important in primary grades, where this information is used often in Math

04
Bulletin Board
Labels

Details are very important. Make sure that boards are neat and presentable. Use the **Bulletin Board Planner** template to help you create top-notch bulletin boards for your classroom.

05
Bulletin Board
Planner

Disorganized boards make a bad first impression on students, parents, and administrators. To create great bulletin boards, follow these steps:

1 · **Plan it.** What boards do you want? Where will you place the boards? Are they accessible (for example, the class news board near the front of the classroom and curricular boards close to learning centers)? Do you have all the materials and supplies you need?

- Backing (paper or fabric)
- Borders
- Construction paper (to frame work)
- Decorative cutouts
- Markers
- Pushpins
- Scissors
- Sentence strips
- Standards
- Stapler and staples
- Yardstick

2 · **Back it.** Select an appropriate color for the backing. Fadeless paper from a teacher supply store is a great option, because it fits the width of the board and lasts a long time (perhaps several years). Other options include fabric, butcher paper (supplied by your school), wallpaper, newspapers and magazines, calendar pictures, and collaged construction paper.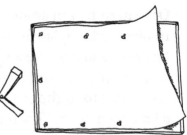

Start at one corner, pinning the backing in place and smoothing out any wrinkles. To flatten the backing, drag a yardstick across the board as you go. Once the backing has been pinned in place, cut off the excess and staple it along the edges; remove the pins. Keep in mind that a border will cover the edges, so they don't have to be perfectly neat. It is important to keep the backing fairly simple, so that student work stands out. You might select a complementary color of construction paper to use as backing for individual pieces of student work, cut so that an even border frames each piece. This creates a cohesive display.

3 · **Frame it.** Teacher supply stores sell a variety of borders. Select an appropriate border to frame the bulletin board, one that coordinates well with the backing. Select a theme-related border that reflects the theme of your current unit, or consider having students create a theme-related border on sentence strips. Other possibilities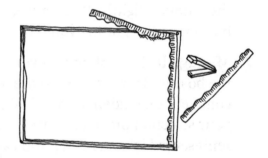

include paper money, postcards, and plastic plant leaves and flowers. Remember that the goal is to display student work or other important information. If you create a board that is too cluttered or busy, you defeat its purpose.

4 · **Label it.** Label the bulletin board so that its purpose is obvious. Most boards have the following features:

- **Title**—"Class News," "Science," "Math," or "Volcanoes"
- **Question**—Include an open-ended question that invites the viewer to think about the posted material. "How" questions work well, because they elicit more than a yes/no answer.
- **Standards**—Select one to three skill standards or learning objectives that are demonstrated in the posted material. Standards should be written in a student-friendly manner. Check with your school about expectations for bulletin boards.
- **Rubric**—A four-point rubric gives students clear expectations. A score of "4" means that expectations have been met, with fewer expectations being met as a score approaches "1."

5 · **Organize it.** Pin students' work in place, adding labels as needed. Position and adjust each piece using a single pushpin until you have optimized the space and have a balanced board. Then pin each item at all four corners. (Staples are harder to remove and are more destructive of the backing.)

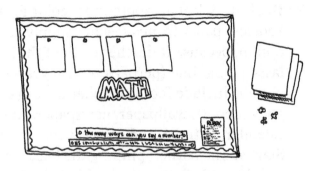

6 · **Pop it.** You can take your board to another level by adding decorative cutouts that relate to an assignment, theme, or curricular area. Students can make these or you can purchase them. A 3-D effect is achieved by bowing the cutouts slightly. Be creative, but remember not to overdo it.

7 · **Manage it.** How often will you change the boards? How will you score and comment on students' work? What is your selection process? Is every student represented in some way? You can mount plastic sleeves on a board, so that papers can be slid in and out as student work is rotated on the board. For writing, consider posting all drafts of a paper, with the final draft on top, so the viewer can see all phases of the writing process. It is important that students understand their score, why they received the score, and ways to improve on that score in the future. Start with a positive comment, and then note an area for improvement. Use Post-it Notes. Your students' best work should be posted—something they are proud of. This is their best work, not necessarily their top-scoring work. You may select a student's best work, or you can allow the student to choose it. Try to have work from all students represented.

8 · **Laminate it**. Laminate what you have created, if you think you may want to use it year after year.

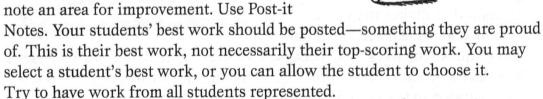

Physical Classroom Setup

Furniture and equipment need to be easily accessible, but they must also be arranged so that you can move around the classroom with ease. Students should be able to see you, and you should be able to see them.

Before going through the process of physically setting up the furniture and equipment in your classroom, walk around the classroom and take into account all of the major components.

- Teacher's desk
- Student desks
- Chairs
- Tables
- Carts
- File cabinets
- Bookcases
- Computer tables
- Other furniture
- Rugs
- Sink
- Doors
- Windows
- Emergency exit
- Closet
- Bulletin boards
- Electrical outlets

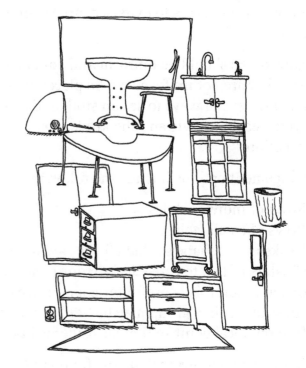

In order to maximize space and efficiency, consider the location and number of each of these items. Use the **Classroom Map** template, either as presented or with graph paper, to design your classroom setup.

08
Classroom
Map

Instructional Focal Point

Where will your primary instruction take place? This must be established first, and the physical organization of the classroom will follow. In this area, you should probably have a whiteboard, electrical outlets, a rug area, and—for primary grades—a calendar bulletin board.

This focal point should allow all students to have full and equal access to the instruction that is delivered there. Traffic patterns must be established to facilitate transitions to and from this area.

Arrangement of Student Desks

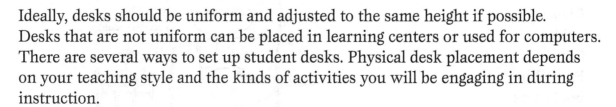

Once the instructional focal point is established,
you will decide where student desks should be placed.
Your arrangement should do the following:

- Provide equal access to the curriculum
- Facilitate multiple learning opportunities
- Facilitate instruction, including teacher observation and support
- Provide easy access to exits, learning centers, rug areas, supplies, closets, and the sink

Ideally, desks should be uniform and adjusted to the same height if possible. Desks that are not uniform can be placed in learning centers or used for computers. There are several ways to set up student desks. Physical desk placement depends on your teaching style and the kinds of activities you will be engaging in during instruction.

Arrangement options include the following:

- Rows of individual desks
- Rows of small tables
- Desks in a U shape so that all eyes are directed toward the whiteboard
- Clusters of two to three desks (four to six students) so that students are facing one another; this is useful for cooperative or small group activities. More than six students in a group may be hard to manage. Remember that clusters should face the focal point so that all students have access to instruction.

Other considerations include the following:

- An appropriate number of chairs for desks
- The same style and size of chairs, if possible
- Placing tennis balls on the feet of heavy chairs to reduce noise and facilitate movement

Remember that the arrangement of student desks can change over time as your teaching changes.

Seating arrangement is critical to optimizing instruction. Assigned seats will change over time, with adjustments made as needed, but when you're starting out, keep these points in mind:

- Even when students have their choice of seating, it is important to have guidelines that permit you to make changes. This can be a good way to start the year until you get to know the students.
- Establishing a schedule for periodic seat changes (every week or every month, for example) allows you to make changes that may be needed because of behavior or learning issues. Students with behavior issues can be separated,

and students needing more instructional support can be moved closer to the front of the class.

- Having assigned seating can avoid the issue of students sitting next to their friends. Student success may suffer when friends have their desks next to one another.

- Having seating available for extra or displaced students is also a good idea. Depending on your district's policy, you could receive extra students for an unfilled substitute assignment of a co-worker's class. These students need desks that they can use for the day and that give them access to instruction. Learning center desks can work well for this purpose. Knowing ahead of time that you are prepared to handle extra students will make it easier to incorporate them into your classroom when the need presents itself.

- It is a good idea to add two more seats to your classroom than the maximum number of students you could potentially be assigned. In the event that you have a full class, room for growth is desirable; at times, your school may have to exceed the maximum number of students. These extra seats can also be used for extra students that may be assigned to you for the day.

Placement of Teacher's Desk

Teachers rarely find time to sit down at their desks during the school day except before and after school, when grading papers, or when preparing lesson plans. Some teachers may opt not to have a desk at all; a bookcase or a student desk  can serve as a place for the teacher to work from. There are several things to consider when you choose the place for your desk.

- Teacher's desk placed close to the main instruction area
    - This placement enables you to face the class directly.
    - Instructional materials and supplies, as well as teacher supplies, are stored in the desk.
    - The desk serves as the focal point for class business.
- Teacher's desk placed at the side or back of the classroom
    - This placement enables you to face the class from the side or back.
    - Teacher supplies are stored in the desk.
    - A separate teacher station for instructional materials and supplies is needed near the front of the classroom.
    - One-on-one conferencing works well with this arrangement.

It is important to create and maintain an arrangement that allows you to readily access all the materials and supplies that you need. Here are a few suggestions:

- Desktop
  - Place items here that are frequently used, such as a calendar blotter, stapler, tape, teacher's editions, plan book, grade book, Post-it Notes, and timer.
- Top drawer
  - Place items here that are frequently used, but should be secured, such as pens, pencils, staples, rubber bands, referral forms, stickers, scissors, glue sticks, and substitute contact cards or flyers.
- First side drawer
  - Store items here that are not needed often, such as extra markers, pencils, pens, and notes or correspondences from home (in a file folder).
- Additional drawers
  - Store items here that are not needed on a daily basis but that still need to be available and secured, such as assessment plans, personal items, confiscated items, and student lists or phone contacts.

File Cabinets

Organizing your instructional resources in a file cabinet is very important. These files can serve as an alternative—or a complement—to the items that are stored in the teacher's desk. You will need to set up a logical system that works well for you.

Instructional Files

- Science units
- Math units
- Reading instruction
- Writing
- Social Studies units
- Multicultural celebrations
- Holidays

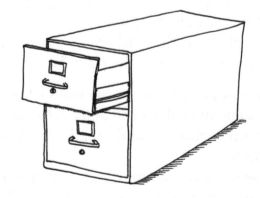

Personal Files

- Agenda files
- Formal lesson plans
- Credential file
- Evaluation file

Student Files

- Assessments
- Anecdotal records

Equipment

Instruction today depends more and more on technology. Teachers use laptops, document readers, SMART Boards, and Senteo interactive systems. Having this equipment available and operational will enhance the instruction in your classroom.

Consider the following as you plan to incorporate equipment in your classroom:

- Store equipment in a safe place (for example, in a locked closet) when it's not being used.
- Designate an area such as a specific desk or table that is always available for equipment. Make sure it is near an electrical outlet and, if projection is required, near a SMART Board or screen.
- Have all support supplies available. For example, overhead markers, a spray bottle with water, and paper towels are all important for use with an overhead projector, and specific cables may be needed to connect projectors to laptops.
- Test equipment and learn how to operate it before using it for the first time with your class. Practice setting it up, using it, and storing it. Know how to use the individual remote controls.
- Keep an inventory of your equipment. At the end of the school year, you may be asked to submit an inventory of the equipment assigned to you or your classroom. Use the **Equipment Inventory** template for this purpose.
- If equipment malfunctions, allow it to cool down before you take further action. Many projectors have a built-in safety device that shuts them down when they overheat. Turning the lamp off or unplugging the projector for a short time may resolve the problem, making it unnecessary to replace an expensive bulb or label the equipment as broken.
- Upper grade students can be trained to set up and take down equipment. This gives them valuable experience and teaches responsibility.

13
Equipment
Inventory

Your classroom equipment may include the following:

- Television—If your school has access to cable or satellite, confirm the channels that are available.
- DVD player—Make sure the DVD player is connected to the television correctly and that it plays a DVD properly.
- CD player—Turn the CD player on, adjust the volume, and make sure that a CD plays properly.
- ELMOs, document readers, projectors, and overhead projectors—Make sure that lightbulbs are in working order and that the equipment can focus. Make sure that cables and adapters connect to a laptop computer, if necessary.

- Computers—Turn each computer on and make sure it is operational. Check Internet access, if available. Check printer connections, if applicable.
- Pencil sharpener—If the sharpener is electric, place it near an electrical outlet. Check to make sure there is no blockage. To avoid excessive use of (and potential damage to) the sharpener, consider appointing a monitor to sharpen pencils weekly. Keep a box with sharpened pencils available so that students can exchange broken pencils for sharpened ones.

Bookcases

Classroom bookcases house teacher's books, student textbooks, dictionaries and reference books, and library books. Strategic placement and organization of bookcases greatly enhance classroom management.

- Bookcases should not interfere with traffic patterns or the ability to observe all students at all times.
- Bookcases with wheels or plastic glider buttons are relatively easy to move.
- Little-used bookcases should be placed out of the way, perhaps along the back wall of the classroom.

Bookcase Options

- Teacher's books
  - Education and resource books
  - Teacher's editions
- Student textbooks
  - A separate bookshelf for each subject
- Books organized by subject area
  - Subject resource books
  - Dictionaries and reference books
  - Extra student textbooks
- Classroom library books
  - Three bookcases in a U shape or several bookcases in an L shape with a rug in the middle create a great classroom library.
  - Beanbag chairs, large pillows, and stuffed animals can create an inviting environment.
  - Books can be placed in tubs or bins that are labeled by subject, such as Plants, Community, and Math. The **Library Labels** template can be used for labeling shelves, tubs, or bins.
  - Colored stickers can be used to indicate the reading level of individual books: For example, red dots indicate "advanced," blue dots "intermediate," and green dots "primary."

22
Library Labels

Small Group Instruction Areas

It is important to have a designated area where the teacher can meet with individual students or small groups of students in order to help them with a specific skill, project, or discussion. This is especially important in the primary grades.

- Set up this area so that you can still see the rest of the class when you are meeting with the smaller group. Place your chair so that you face the students you are working with, as well as the rest of the class (for example, students at their desks or at centers).
- If you choose not to have a small table and chairs for this small group instruction, you can use a rug area or form a small circle with student chairs.
- If you have more than one small group working cooperatively at the same time, be clear about who meets where.
- Place work folders near this area so that students can easily access materials for ongoing projects.
- Even if you have a teacher supply kit, consider creating a separate kit for this area, containing supplies that support these specific activities.

Teacher Supplies

- Pens, pencils, and markers
- Post-it Notes
- Scissors
- Stapler and staples
- Tape
- Glue sticks
- Paper clips

Learning Materials

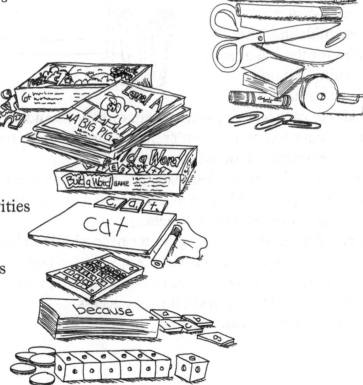

- Leveled readers
- Learning games and activities
- Small whiteboards
- Calculators
- Word cards and letter tiles
- Math manipulatives
- Puzzles

Student supplies that are used in the group can also be kept in this area. Plastic boxes with lids provide great storage and are easy to stack. While students could bring their own supplies to this area, this might become problematic if supplies are lost or misplaced.

Student Supplies

- Pencils, markers, and crayons
- Paper (for writing and drawing)
- Scissors
- Glue sticks

Learning Centers

Learning centers are excellent ways for students to apply what they have learned. It is essential to set up centers so that students can work at them independently.

- Give students an orientation to the specific guidelines and expectations related to each learning center. Introduce activities one at a time, and gradually increase the options at each center.
- Post guidelines and rules for the use of each learning center.
- Consider having a file folder at each learning center with directions and a materials list.
- If you have a computer center, make sure the monitors are positioned so you can see what the students are working on.
- Make sure that all needed materials are available at a curricular center (such as for writing or math) or an activity center, so that students do not have to leave the center in search of materials.
- If possible, locate a learning center near a bulletin board or bookcase that is specific to that center's curricular area or activity.
- Student desks can be used as learning centers, with materials in containers that are stored in the desks for easy access.
- Student monitors can maintain the centers.

Textbooks

Textbooks are assigned to students, who are responsible for the books that have been issued to them. An organized system of assigning books, dealing with lost books, and storing extra books is important for good classroom management. The **Textbook Inventory** and **Textbook Sign-Out Sheet** templates can be used for this purpose. There are several issues to consider.

46
Textbook
Inventory
47
Textbook
Sign-Out
Sheet

- Are textbooks to be kept at school, or are students allowed to take them home?
- If there is room, textbooks can be kept in student desks. If there is not enough room in the desks, consider keeping textbooks in a designated bookcase.
- Consider keeping textbooks that aren't used on a daily basis in a designated bookcase.
- Keep extra textbooks in a designated bookcase or on a closet shelf. Secure them so that students don't help themselves to new books when books have been lost.

- Review guidelines and expectations for the care of textbooks with your students.

Instructional Materials

There are many supplemental materials, workbooks, and manipulatives that support adopted curricular series. Keeping these materials organized and readily available helps a classroom run smoothly.

- Consumable workbooks are assigned to individual students. Extra copies should be stored with their companion textbooks in a secure place.
- Teacher resource books that accompany teacher's editions should be kept in a designated area (for instance, a Science bookshelf or Math bookshelf). Be sure that these materials are visible and easily accessible.
- Manipulatives for Math can be stored in containers and kept with the Math resources. Students need to be introduced to them prior to their use, and guidelines for their use should be reviewed.
- Science materials and supplies should be stored in a secure location, often in a designated closet. Plastic containers and zipper bags are ideal for storage; these should be organized and labeled for easy access.
- Additional materials and supplies (for example, dictionaries, thesauruses, maps, and learning games) can be placed either strategically in the classroom or in a designated area, closet, or bookcase. All of these materials should be easily accessible to the students and the teacher.

Student Work and Student Portfolios

"In" and "Out" baskets facilitate collecting and distributing student work, such as homework, spelling tests, and math quizzes. Students put their work into the "In" basket upon completion, and they pick it up from the "Out" basket after it has been graded and is ready to be returned.

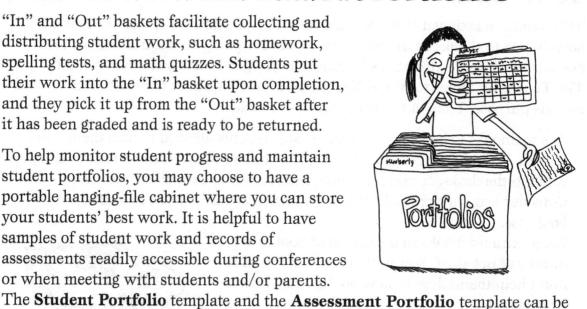

To help monitor student progress and maintain student portfolios, you may choose to have a portable hanging-file cabinet where you can store your students' best work. It is helpful to have samples of student work and records of assessments readily accessible during conferences or when meeting with students and/or parents.

43
Student
Portfolio

02
Assessment
Portfolio

The **Student Portfolio** template and the **Assessment Portfolio** template can be used to help organize student work and assessments accessed in these meetings.

Utilizing Storage Space

A classroom must be free of clutter. Both the teacher and the students function better in an organized and tidy environment.

Closets

A closet may be available to house the supplies that you have in bulk, as well as extra items that you need but may not have to access on a daily basis. Think of this closet as your warehouse. Stock the closet with a supply of pencils and paper. Anticipate your needs so that you can avoid a last-minute rush for many of these supplies—red and green paper at Christmas, for example, or No. 2 pencils with erasers for testing. Be sure to keep the closet organized so that you know what you have and can easily access it.

- Consider designating a particular closet or specific shelves in a closet for specific curricular areas (for example, the Art closet or the Science shelf).
- Store frequently used items at eye level, if possible.

- Place items that are used infrequently (such as liquid starch or watercolor paints) on either a high or low shelf.
- Place heavy items (such as boxes of paper and magazines) on either a low shelf or the floor.
- Organize small supplies in plastic containers with lids (purchased at discount stores) that can be labeled.
- Consider storing some frequently used supplies in a movable cart with drawers.

Here is a list of items you may wish to consider having on hand but stored away:

- Extra pencils, colored pencils, markers, pens, and crayons
- Writing paper
- Colored construction paper
- Scratch paper, such as newsprint
- Lined tag or poster paper
- Sentence strips and word cards
- Scissors
- Glue
- Glue sticks
- Tape
- Brad fasteners
- File folders
- Art materials
  - Special papers (such as tissue paper)
  - Pastels, including oil pastels
  - Drawing chalk
  - Yarn and cord
  - Paints (which could also be stored in the sink area)

Don't be greedy! Teachers sometimes fall into a "hoarding trap" and overstock their supplies, creating chaos. Streamline your storage, and trust that you will have the supplies you need when you need them.

You might find it helpful to give parents a list of supplies you want your students to have during the school year. Because any material sent home should be approved by the school, be sure to clear this with your school or district.

The Sink Area

In the sink area, there is usually storage below the sink and sometimes above it in a wall cabinet. This is where you should keep cleaning products, and it is a good place to store liquid art supplies, such as paint and starch. Other art supplies that require clean-up at the sink, such as paintbrushes, are also logically stored in the sink area.

- Keep the sink area clean and sanitary.
- Keep in mind that a drinking fountain is often located in the sink area, and it must be kept clean.
- Make sure there are no leaks at either the faucet or the pipes under the sink.
- Store liquid art supplies, such as paints and starch, and other related art supplies like paintbrushes in the sink area.
- Store approved cleansers, sponges, and paper towels in the sink area.
- Keep the first aid kit near the sink; generally, scrapes and cuts need to be washed before a Band-Aid is applied.

Students' Belongings

The areas where students' belongings are stored should be well organized and easily accessible. It is important to consider traffic patterns to and from these areas in order to make things run smoothly when students put their belongings away or retrieve them.

- Designate the area where students hang their coats and backpacks. Storing these items outside the instructional area keeps the classroom neat and tidy. It can be distracting to have these items on the backs of chairs, although upper grade classrooms may use this option.
- Keep lunches and/or snacks in a sturdy plastic box, perhaps at the classroom door or near the sink area. Lunches and snacks should always be labeled to avoid conflicts; consider putting a student monitor in charge of the area.
- Designate a place in the classroom where students place lost-and-found items. If the classroom is self-contained, this may not be necessary.
- Physical education equipment belonging to your class can be stored in a plastic tub or a ball bag. A student monitor can supervise equipment checkout and return.

Efficiency Is the Key

Be creative when setting up your classroom, but most important, be practical. Make your classroom a place that functions well for you and your students. Organize it so that it is efficient and facilitates learning. Keep in mind that you are all there together for a very large part of each day, and your classroom should be a place that is welcoming and inviting to you, your students, and their parents.

3 Establishing Rules, Consequences, and Procedures

Once the physical environment of your classroom has been set up, with its space organized for efficiency and facilitation of learning, you will want to consider how rules, consequences, and procedures are established for the classroom. Rules and consequences, together with procedures, create an orderly environment that enables a classroom to run efficiently, and they establish the expectations for behavior. Therefore, it is important to come up with a system that communicates your expectations. You should work with your students so they understand what behaviors you expect and can practice them. It is also important to make sure that there is an opportunity for your students' concerns to be recognized. This chapter introduces several ways to include your students in establishing rules, consequences, and procedures for the classroom.

Consider the following:

- The ideal classroom runs smoothly: Disruptions and wasted time are minimized, and opportunities for student learning are maximized.
- It is difficult for a teacher to conduct instruction and for students to work productively if there are no guidelines for behavior in the classroom.
- When students don't behave according to established guidelines for behavior, they must have a clear understanding of the consequences of their behavior.

Establishing Classroom Rules

A set of three to five rules should be sufficient to cover the most important areas of behavior. Having a few comprehensive rules is much more effective than having many specific rules. Fewer rules are easier to remember and are more "doable." As students get older, additional rules that deal with specific behaviors can be used.

It is important to state rules in a positive manner whenever possible. For example, "Do not hit," "Do not take another student's pencil," "Don't kick another student," and "No fighting" can all be stated as "Keep your hands and feet to yourself." Remember that focusing on the positive is always more effective.

You should know ahead of time what general rules you think are appropriate for your classroom, but it is important to include your students in creating the list of rules and consequences that govern the classroom. When students help create the classroom rules, it gives them buy-in and ownership. This helps eliminate many arguments about the rules that might otherwise occur: When a student is called out because of his or her inappropriate behavior, you can simply point to the rules. During the discussion establishing rules for the classroom, you can ask questions that will steer the process toward rules you are comfortable with.

Having clear, consistent consequences to accompany the rules that govern your classroom is a necessity. Consequences should build from less severe to more severe. There should be a penalty for the student who makes a mistake or two, but it shouldn't involve anything as serious as a trip to the office or a call home. If you show consistent follow-through when dealing with rules and consequences, the students will develop trust and confidence in your leadership in the classroom. This cannot be stressed enough. When students know that you adhere to the classroom guidelines consistently, they are more likely to realize it is because of their own choices that they are disciplined for not following a classroom rule.

Following are some general rules, organized by grade level, that encompass many areas of behavior in the classroom. Rules such as these are often found in well-managed classrooms. The **Rule Planner** template can be used to help you set up your own classroom guidelines.

26
Rule Planner

Kindergarten–First Grade

- Raise your hand.
- Keep your hands and feet to yourself.
- Walk.
- Treat other people the way you would like to be treated.
- Follow directions.

Second-Third Grades

- Follow directions the first time.
- Raise your hand and wait for permission to talk.
- Stay in your seat while the teacher is teaching.
- Keep hands, feet, and objects to yourself.
- Respect yourself and others.

Fourth-Sixth Grades

- Pay attention and listen carefully.
- Raise your hand to be heard.
- Stay focused, and stay on task.
- Keep hands and objects to yourself.
- Keep your desk area clean and organized.

Secondary Grades or Advanced Learners

- Follow directions the first time.
- Speak appropriately to adults and peers.
- Use only given names. (For example, use "Sam," not "Dawg.")
- Avoid name-calling and teasing.
- Avoid verbal abuse or threats to others.
- Behave appropriately.
- Avoid physical or verbal disruptions.

Rules That Work for Any Grade

- Be responsible.
- Be respectful of others and their property.
- Keep your hands and feet to yourself.
- Listen carefully and follow directions.
- Have a positive attitude.
- Do your best.

Additional Ideas for Rules

- Respect others' personal space.
- Respect the rights and property of others.
- Come to class with all supplies.
- Come to class with your homework completed.
- Complete all assignments neatly and on time.
- Listen quietly while others are speaking.
- Raise your hand and wait to be called on.
- Leave your seat only when necessary.
- Leave your seat only with permission.
- Be quiet in lines, hallways, and restrooms.
- Respect your classmates, teachers, and other adults.
- Stay on task.
- Always do your best.
- Obey all school rules.
- Help those in need.

It is important to establish rules that work for you. If you are new to teaching, the rules that we suggest are a good place to start. Keep in mind that the process of establishing classroom rules may take several days. Ultimately, however, you have the final say about which rules are established. It is important to consider the diversity of your students (including cultural background, special needs, learning styles, and language ability) when making these final decisions. And remember, always present whatever rules you and your students create in a positive manner.

Classroom management theorists have stated that while student involvement in establishing classroom rules is important, the students' input can be handled in many different ways. Students' voices can be heard if you give them an opportunity to express their thoughts about things that concern them in the classroom and on the playground. This can be done through "Tattle Time," a "Friendly Letter," or a "Comment Box." Each of these gives students a chance to voice their concerns, and they all provide an excellent opportunity for students to practice putting their thoughts into writing. The **Comments and Suggestions Slips** template can be used for this purpose.

09
Comments
and
Suggestions
Slips

Establishing Classroom Consequences

To be effective, consequences must be imposed consistently. Choose consequences that are appropriate and that work for your particular class. When determining what consequences are appropriate for your classroom, consider the following:

- First and foremost, make sure that you know the policy guidelines for your school and/or district.
- Ask other teachers about the behavior management system they use in their classrooms. Your style may be different, but you can get some useful ideas.
- Not all consequences that you observe being used by another teacher should be emulated with your students.
- Ask yourself, "Would I appreciate a situation being handled this way if this were my child?" Consider, "If an administrator or the Evening News were in the room, would I handle this situation in the same way?"
- Ask, "Am I being consistent and fair with this student?"
- Always conduct yourself with integrity and professionalism.

It is important to establish a hierarchy of consequences and follow through with them consistently. Here are some suggested consequences:

1 · **First Offense**—Warning
2 · **Second Offense**—Time-out from an activity (primary grades) or detention (upper grades)
3 · **Third Offense**—Communication home: note (to be signed and returned), phone call, or e-mail
4 · **Fourth Offense**— Action plan recorded with the office and/or counselor
5 · **Fifth Offense**— Conference with parents, the teacher, and an administrator at school

Time-Out

A time-out is a short time away from the group to calm down—one minute per year of the student's age is a good way to determine the length of time used for a time-out. For example, a six-year-old could be assigned a six-minute time-out.

- A student who is easily distracted may respond better to shorter time-outs.
- You may want to designate a specific area with no distractions for time-outs.
- Sometimes, a student needs a more complete break from the group and is sent to another classroom.
  - Prior arrangements must be made with the receiving teacher.
  - The student should leave with work in hand and for only the designated time-out period.
- It is not acceptable to send students to stand in a corner or outside the classroom.

Detention

Detention is typically used at the junior high and high school levels, although primary schools might consider imposing detention during recess, depending on grade level. Teachers can take turns monitoring these sessions. Make sure you know the school's policies for detention and follow them.

Communication Home

Use a communication home when the student's behavior warrants it, for example, if inappropriate behavior is consistent and no resolution is in sight. Parents are busy, so be sure not to send communications home for minor behavior problems. However, parents don't appreciate being blindsided by a call from an administrator to set up a meeting about a behavior issue that they know nothing about. As the teacher, you need to follow through on every phone call or e-mail home. You see only part of the picture when you observe that child in your classroom. You may be able to deal with inappropriate behavior better if you know where it comes from. The **Student Contact Information** template can be used for this purpose.

39
Student
Contact
Information

Action Plan and/or Conference

Be sure to keep careful documentation about your students' behavior, and make sure that you save all notes. These teacher records serve as evidence of your students' behavior, as well as how you have handled it in the classroom.

Summary

As the teacher, it is you who sets the example and helps students understand that their actions have consequences—not only for themselves, but also for the class and, by extension, the community. Students have choices. It is your job to help them understand this and to equip them to make appropriate choices in life.

Establishing Classroom Procedures

Use of Classroom Elements

It is important to establish well thought-out procedures to regulate use of the many elements in your classroom. Anticipate areas that need established boundaries in order to head off potential problems. Consider the following classroom elements and the recommendations for regulating them.

Teacher's Desk

Students may not remove anything from your desk or personal bookcases without your permission.

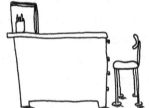

Student Desks

Students may not bother other students' desks. Set aside time every week for your students to clean and organize their books, other learning materials, and supplies. If two students share a desk, have them divide the desk in half, with each student taking a side.

Storage of Supplies and Resources

- Classroom supplies and resources can be stored on shelves, in drawers, in closets, or in cabinets. Consider storing items that could be distracting and problematic behind closed doors. This includes markers, glue, scissors, and pastels.
- It is important to establish procedures for using these materials—when they may be used and whether or not permission is needed to access them. Practice these procedures, for example, by having designated monitors pass items out and then collect them. A routine keeps the classroom running smoothly. This is especially important for primary students.

Drinking Water

- School policy may allow students to keep water bottles at their seats, and you may feel comfortable allowing that in your classroom. If so, make it clear that sharing from bottles is not allowed. (Avoid juices or other drinks that can create a sticky mess if spilled.)
- Students may be permitted to go to the drinking fountain quietly, one at a time, when you are not delivering instruction.
- You may decide not to permit drinking water at all during class.

The Sink

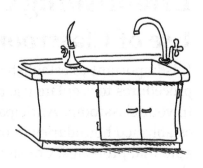

- The sink is used for washing hands and cleaning up, as well as for storage of specific art and/or cleaning supplies.
- Students should have permission to access the sink.
- You may want to designate a student monitor to keep the sink area clean and retrieve needed items from that area.

The Pencil Sharpener

- Pencil sharpening should not occur during instructional time—when you are teaching or while students are working.
- A student monitor can be designated to sharpen pencils and supervise an exchange when a broken pencil is returned.
- Storing the pencil sharpener after each use is a good idea in order to avoid distraction during class.

Learning Centers and Activity Centers

Learning and activity centers can be fun and engaging, but they can also be an easy distraction for students. Procedures must be established to maximize their benefits and minimize their distractions.

06
Center
Sign-In Sheet

07
Center
Tracker

- Introduce center activities and practice them with students before making a new center available to the class.
- Establish a system for the use of centers on a rotation basis. A timer can be used to control the rotation. The **Center Sign-In Sheet** and the **Center Tracker** templates can be used for this purpose.
- Have students practice rotating through the centers. This is especially important for primary students. You may want to literally walk them through the rotation several times.
- Color-coded groups, numbered groups, or names on clothespins are all good ways to organize student rotations. Any of these systems will allow students to know when it is their turn to use a center.
- A designated monitor can assist in supervising the centers and the center rotation.

Classroom Computers

Computer use should be structured. Procedures must be established, whether computers are being used for educational games, research activity, or the preparation of documents.

- Monitor computer use and establish a rotation system for student use.
- Check with colleagues to find out how they incorporate computers in the classroom.
- Most districts have a firewall to prevent students from accessing inappropriate websites, but some students may be able to circumvent it. Remind students about websites that they are allowed to access, and monitor your students when they are working at the computers.

Heat and Air Conditioning

Only the teacher or a designated student should adjust the thermostat in the classroom.

Door, Telephone, and Intercom

- You may want to assign a monitor to answer the door or telephone. This is an excellent way to avoid a rush to either one by several students.
- Teach students how to properly answer the phone: "Room _____, [name of student] speaking" or "Good morning, this is Room _____."

Student Participation

You must identify ways to allow all students to ask questions, contribute to a discussion, and receive help. Teachers may tend to call on the same students without being aware of it, but it is important not to fall into this habit. Make a point to call on every student, giving everyone a chance to participate in the lesson. There are several ways to call on your students:

- Students may raise their hand for recognition by the teacher.
- Students may call on the next student responder.

- Students may give a specific signal to indicate they have a question or comment.
- Students may toss a beanbag or soft ball to the next student responder.
- You may draw names from a box until everyone has been called on. If a student cannot answer, place that student's name back in the box so it can be drawn later. The **Student Name Cards** and **Student Name Strips** templates can be used for this purpose.
- Names can be written on Popsicle sticks, index cards, or playing cards.
- Names can be checked off a class list.
- The whole class may answer together in a choral response.

41
Student Name
Cards
42
Student Name
Strips

Talking Among Students

Talking quietly is an important part of many activities. This is especially true if you have English language learners in your classroom. Offering opportunities for English language learners to use academic English is critical for their language development, and a "silent" classroom is not one where English language development occurs.

Students must know when and how loudly they may talk. If you allow students to talk to one another as they work together during individual work activities, it is necessary to establish specific limitations. You must decide how much noise is acceptable for students working at centers and in groups. Your goal is to have "productive talk," where students are sharing and learning from each other at a controlled sound volume.

Several ways that students can have "productive talk" follow:

- Whispering, or using "inside voices"
- Think-Pair-Share (Two students reflect on a topic or issue, and then discuss it.)
- Knees to Knees (Two students face each other so they can speak quietly.)
- Shoulder to Shoulder (Two students sit next to one another so they can speak quietly.)
- Quiet chatter (a quiet, productive level of talking)
- Small cooperative groups (Several students work together, using productive talk to share and develop information.)

Many teachers find it helpful to have a "zero noise" signal for times when they need the whole class to get completely quiet. It is important not to overuse this signal, because it can become ineffective. When your signal is given, you need to honor it and follow through. If you model it for your students consistently, it will be effective. Here are some ideas for signaling "zero noise":

- Hold two fingers of one hand up, while holding the other two fingers over the mouth.
- Hold a "quiet" hand up; students respond with a "quiet" hand up until everyone is quiet.
- Ring a bell (just a few short rings).
- Count down—from five to one, for example, or from ten to one.
- Clap a pattern. Students respond by repeating the clapped pattern.
- Turn on music.

Obtaining Help

When students are working at their seats and they need your help, it can be distracting to other students or to you if they call out or approach you, interrupting the task at hand.

Develop a system or signal that allows your students to tell you that they need help, but that avoids students' waiting with their hand up. Suggestions for systems or signals that allow students to get help follow:

- Use a system of green, blue, and red poker chips. Green means they don't need help, blue means to stop by, and red means they can't continue their work without help.
- Use restaurant table number holders for "help" signs. Each student has three colored cards for the holder: one for "no help needed," one for "I could use help," and one for "I can't continue my work without help."
- Have students quietly ask two nearby friends for help before they ask for help from the teacher. If students are encouraged to help each other, you will need a system to regulate when that's appropriate and how it should be handled.
- Teach your students to move to the next question, activity, or sentence while they wait for help. Otherwise, the period may come to an end before you can help them, and the student will get no work done.
- If you choose to help students at a place in the classroom other than their desks, choose a location that allows you to observe the rest of the class.

Activities for "Early Finishers"

Some students will finish their work earlier than others. Always have an additional enrichment or challenge activity available for these students that relates to what they just finished. For example, make five extra copies of activities throughout the year,

so that early finishers can go to the "Extra Work" basket and select a previously assigned page as a review. For a greater challenge, check your curriculum for additional activities or purchase an activity book for the next grade level. These can be copied and placed in a "Challenge" basket. Doing this ensures that early finishers will have purposeful options that are engaging and not a waste of time. Students who finish their work early may do one of the following:

- Read silently.
- Complete an ongoing project.
- Work at a center.
- Play an academic game.
- Work on a puzzle, like Sudoku.
- Work on a sheet from the "Extra Work" basket.
- Work on a sheet from the "Challenge" basket.

Classroom Transitions

Beginning the School Day

The start of the school day sets the stage for the rest of the day. Be sure you begin the day in your classroom in a positive and upbeat way. The students will pick up on your energy, so it is you who determines the tone of the school day. Because consistency and routine offer security to students, it is important to establish a routine to open each day in your classroom.

- Have students put their backpacks in the designated area. Establish a system, perhaps five students at a time after everyone has entered the classroom.
- Have students place their lunches and/or snacks in the designated area.

76

- Have students take out the necessary materials for the first period.
  - Homework (if checked at their seats)
  - Pencil and paper
  - Textbook
- Have students place homework or homework folders in a designated bin (if graded later by the teacher).
- Take attendance. (Students may read during this time.)
- Conduct the flag salute.
- Conduct the lunch count, if required.
- Review the day's agenda.
- Conduct a "Do Now" activity for students once they are in their seats.
  - Summarize "what we learned" from a curricular area the previous day for the students to record in their journals.
  - Read from a book of choice or from a selected reading.
  - Work an activity sheet.
  - Work a daily warm-up page.

Leaving the Classroom

Students leave the classroom many times during the day for regular activities such as restroom use, recess, lunch, music class, the computer lab, and the library. How your students leave the classroom is not something to be taken lightly: In an emergency, orderly lines and fast, efficient exiting could save lives. Have the class practice leaving as if for an emergency, and follow the proper protocol and route. It is critical to have procedures in place for this.

A Pair of Students Leaving the Classroom

- A designated student monitor should accompany a student leaving the room to go to the restroom, the nurse, or the office. Always have students leave the classroom in pairs—never a student alone. There are liability issues if a student leaves alone, so it is better for the student's own safety to leave the classroom accompanied by another student.
- If a student is being escorted to the office or the nurse and might not return, send two monitors to drop the student off so that they can return as a pair.

77

The Whole Class Leaving the Classroom

- Have the students line up, with the quietest table or row going first.
- Assign a line-up order that students always follow. This can avoid pushing and arguing while they are lining up. Students can more easily line up quickly, which is important in an emergency. It also makes it easy for you to spot who is not present.
- Call the students to line up by row or table in a systematic manner.
- Call the table with the most behavior points to line up first.
- Have students line up according to clothing color, correct response to questions about the day's lessons, or correctly spelling words you call out.
- Have students line up by groups (tables or rows) whose names you pull from a hat.

Other Considerations

- Assign line leaders to organize the lines.
- Rotate the line leader every week so that every student has a chance to be the line leader.
- Have students walk in a straight line, with hands at their sides, and with little or no talking. This makes emergency exits more efficient, and it also reflects well on your class.

Returning to the Classroom

An established procedure for students to enter the room quietly and take their seats limits distractions and saves time. Suggestions for possible procedures include the following:

- With the lights off and quiet music playing as part of a five-minute cool-down, have students return from recess and lunch and put their heads on their desks.
- Post a "Do Now" activity every time students return to the classroom.
- Have students read silently for 10 to 15 minutes before asking them to refocus on classwork.
- Do a warm-up activity, for example, a daily math problem or page that leads into your math lesson.

Routine Classroom Activities

Many routine classroom activities support student learning. Performing these activities quietly and efficiently is important in order to limit distractions. Students should always follow established protocol, such as going to the following areas only when instruction is not taking place, or asking permission first, if that is the established procedure for your classroom.

- The restroom
    - Go in pairs (with a monitor).
    - Do not engage in horseplay.
    - Wash your hands.
    - Leave and return quietly.
- The sink
    - Take turns at the sink area, one student at a time, unless the teacher has specified otherwise.
    - Keep the area neat.
    - Always turn the water off.
    - Do not play in the water.
- The pencil sharpener
    - Take turns at the pencil sharpener, one student at a time.
    - If you take a pencil, you must return one.
    - Always unplug an electric sharpener when emptying it into the trash can.
- The drinking fountain
    - Take turns at the drinking fountain, one student at a time.
    - Count to five for each student's turn, and then rotate to the next student.

Ending the School Day

Briefly review what was covered in class before dismissing your students, especially in the primary grades. An involved parent will ask, "What did you learn in school today?" and a quick review at the end of the school day will help the student be ready with a reply. If you review a curricular area and write about it on the board, the students can write about it as a "Do Now" activity the next day in their journals. This creates documentation of learning and reinforces learning.

Organize the class before permitting anyone to leave, so you are not left to take care of everything. For younger grades, allow plenty of time to get ready to go home. This process will take less and less time as the students get used to your procedures. It is very important to establish a routine for this pre-dismissal time. Some suggestions follow:

- Review homework and model a few examples.
- Have students make sure their desks are clean and organized.
- Assign helpers to assist with clean-up of the room, such as sweeping the room, emptying trash, and erasing the board.
- Assign a helper to put chairs on top of the desks if the floor is to be cleaned.
- Write a summary or review of what was learned so that students can record this in their journals the next morning.
- Hand out paperwork or homework to be sent home. Primary grade students may have homework folders. These can be easily and quickly filled by having designated students each hold an item to be sent home, then selecting and filling one student's folder with the item from each of the designated students. Once the homework folder is filled, the student takes it, gets his backpack, and returns to his seat. Select the next student's folder and continue in this manner until all paperwork and folders are distributed.

You must establish a system for dismissing students at the end of the school day. Know your school's policy and be sure to follow it. Older students are sometimes released from a classroom, while younger students are walked to a designated location to be picked up by parents. It is important to wait with younger students until they have been picked up or loaded onto their assigned bus. Train younger students to say good-bye to you so that you can determine who they are leaving with and make eye contact with that person. Students who have not been picked up should wait in the office until their parents can be notified. It is imperative to follow school dismissal protocol for the safety of your students.

Sometimes a student may leave with a friend or neighbor and be considered "missing." You may be able to avoid this situation by having your students practice dismissal procedures. Some suggested systems for dismissing students at the end of the school day are the following:

- Take the whole class outside as a group.
- Dismiss the whole class from the classroom.
- Dismiss the students based on which tables earned the most points that day.
- Dismiss the students with a game, such as calling out times tables, states and capitals, spelling words, and vocabulary. As students answer correctly, they are dismissed.

General Procedures

The following common school day situations should be considered. You may want to establish routine procedures for your class to ensure that these are handled quickly and easily.

Distributing Materials

- Each week, assign students to be in charge of distributing materials. This avoids arguments over who gets to help the teacher, and it allows quick and easy transitions from subject to subject.
- Designate students as "teaching assistants" or "teacher helpers."

Interruptions and Delays

- Develop strategies for addressing intercom disruptions and/or visits from other adults.
- Have students hold up two fingers as a silent signal to indicate an interruption that must be addressed. This can quiet the class so that the announcement or visit can be tended to quickly. Primary students might be asked to place their hands on top of their heads.

Restroom Breaks

- Know your school's restroom break policy.
- Encourage students to use the restroom before class, at break, at lunch, and after school so as not to interrupt instruction.
- Establish a routine for restroom breaks at other times in the school day, for example, two students go to the restroom together and carry a restroom pass.
- Allow more opportunities for restroom breaks for primary students.
- Have older students pay back any class minutes they missed at the next break.
- In an emergency, allow a student to tell a neighbor and leave quickly with the bathroom monitor to avoid an accident.
- When deciding on your restroom break policy, consider that there is nothing more distracting or uncomfortable for a child than having to go to the bathroom.

The Library

- On the day before your library visit, remind students to bring their books to school with them.
- Have a system for checking out and turning in books, for going to and returning from the library, and for choosing library books while there.

The Resource Room

- If you have students who are taken out of class for additional help, you may want to post a reminder card on their desks listing the days and times they are scheduled to visit resource personnel.

The Office

- Send a referral form with a student who is sent to the office for a referral, or a pass with a student who is sent to drop something off.
- Have a student who is sent to the office for a referral go with two other students, in case the student has to remain in the office. The returning students will return as partners.

The Nurse

- When a student has a medical concern, complete the necessary referral form and send the student to the nurse. Remember, you are not a medical professional.
- Send a referred student to the nurse with two other students. If he or she has to remain with the nurse, the other two students will return as partners.
- Always use gloves to tend to a student who is bleeding, both to model proper first aid procedures and to protect yourself.

The Cafeteria

- Don't assume that students know what is expected of them in the cafeteria. Students need to know where they are supposed to sit, how they are supposed to behave, and how they are supposed

to discard their lunch containers and trash. Teach them specifically what is expected of them in the cafeteria.

The Playground and Equipment

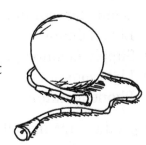

- Students need to know what areas of the playground they can access during recess and after lunch.
- Students should know how to use playground equipment appropriately.
- Students should always return equipment to its proper place.
- If you pick your students up at the playground, meet them at a designated location. Never just call them in.
- Follow school protocol when on the playground.

Fire and Disaster Drills

- Students need specific training about what to do and where to go during a fire drill or disaster drill. This must be practiced several times during the school year.
- Students need to know where the emergency backpack is located.
- Teachers must know their specific role as part of the school disaster response team.
- To limit fire and smoke damage in case of an actual fire, doors are typically closed.

Classroom Helpers and Monitors

- At the beginning of each week, you may want to assign students to handle specific tasks to keep the classroom organized and functioning efficiently.
- Establish a helper or monitor chart that lists the classroom jobs. Students' names can be written on cards and attached with clothespins or paperclips each week for easy rotation. Jobs for students may include the following:
  - Paper monitor
  - Homework monitor
  - Pencil monitor
  - Office monitor
  - Nurse monitor
  - Clean-up monitor
  - Door monitor
  - Trash and/or recycling monitor

- Sweep monitor
- Equipment monitor (to take out and put away balls and jump rope, for example)
- Board monitor (to erase the board)
- Computer monitor (to turn computers on and off)
- Line monitor
- Supply monitor (to pass out supplies)
- Light monitor
- Phone monitor

25
Procedures
Log

It is good to organize all of these procedures in one spot. The **Procedures Log** template can be used for this purpose. Having procedures organized will be extremely helpful when you need to leave plans for a substitute teacher, share them with your administrator, or use them for conferencing with parents.

Managing Student Behavior

With rules, consequences, and procedures in place, your classroom environment is orderly and can run efficiently. For the most part, your students follow the established guidelines that they have helped create. You will want to be actively involved in maintaining the students' cooperation with these guidelines in order to sustain appropriate behavior throughout the year.

In every school day, however, something new or unanticipated may occur that makes applying classroom rules and consequences difficult if you are not prepared for it. With this in mind, you should consider ways to be proactive in meeting student behavior issues—both positive and negative—while maintaining consistency in your handling of the classroom.

Good classroom management depends on many factors that come together to create an environment where there are clear expectations and established boundaries for students. These factors include careful planning of the classroom's organization, being ready with initial activities, setting rules and enforcing consequences, establishing procedures, and delivering quality instruction.

In Chapter 1, several theories from leading authorities in classroom management and discipline were introduced. Consider the ideas expressed in each of those educational theories and see if you can determine with whom you identify most closely. Incorporate their ideas into your classroom and develop a personal system of discipline and management of your own. In doing so, be sure to consider your students' individual needs and personalities, as well as the needs of your classroom, the school, and the larger community.

Consistency

One of the most important elements of managing student behavior is consistency in handling situations with your students. Establishing consistency means that you communicate clear expectations for specific desired behaviors and the consequences that result from those behaviors, as well as the consequences that result from undesirable behaviors. It is important that you maintain the same expectations for appropriate behavior at all times, and for all students. A consistent approach avoids confusion and surprises and helps your students know—rather than have to guess—what is acceptable behavior and what is not.

Think about how you want to be treated by your administrator: You undoubtedly prefer to know what is expected and what procedures will be followed. This applies to the students in your class as well. They need to know what behaviors you consider to be appropriate—or inappropriate—in every aspect of their role as students. This includes countless situations throughout the school day, for example, when students may or may not talk, student interaction during specific activities, and independent work time.

Begin by establishing basic ground rules for expectations of appropriate behavior. These include the more obvious aspects of running an orderly classroom:

- Raise your hand.
- Follow directions.
- Listen to the teacher.
- Respect others.

In time, you will want to introduce more rules for your classroom routines. Provide a rationale and explain your expectations clearly for each activity. For example, begin the year with a "work quietly" ground rule. Once students are acclimated to the rules, introduce activities where relevant on-task talking is permitted. Provide a signal that indicates when talking is allowed or when talking needs to end.

Every classroom routine or procedure that you establish provides your students with a way to know what the expectations are for their behavior and what the consequences are for behaving inappropriately in a particular situation. Each one also provides a mechanism for you to handle the situation in a consistent manner.

The first few weeks of the school year could involve a "boot camp" of sorts for your students, where they learn and practice classroom routines and procedures. This may be especially important for students in the primary grades, where it takes more time for students to learn them. All this practice may take a lot of classroom time initially, but in the long term it can save time by creating a very efficient classroom. In this initial period, you may want to establish and teach procedures for the following:

- Entering and exiting the classroom
- Traffic patterns within the classroom—to the rug, to centers, and to small group areas
- Handing out paper, scissors, glue, and other supplies
- Sharpening pencils and exchanging broken ones for new ones
- Using games and puzzles
- Cleaning up
- The morning routine (for example, calendar and attendance)
- Storing and retrieving coats and backpacks
- Collecting and distributing homework
- Daily routines (for example, journals and silent reading)

An experienced kindergarten teacher will have a routine for doing everything in the classroom. It is the only way to manage younger students productively. Younger students love boundaries, and they are the first to tell you if you are doing something wrong. Older students may not be as vocal or need quite as much routine, but they too respond positively to classroom routines.

To help you determine what routines and procedures to establish in your classroom, consider the many activities that occur there during the school day and ask yourself, "How will things be done?" Observe other teachers, and ask them how they handle their classroom activities—everything from passing out paper to distributing homework.

Establishing routines and procedures in your classroom provides a way for you to maintain consistency throughout the school day for your students.

A Positive Classroom Climate

It is very important that the climate for learning be a positive one, so that students *want* to come to class. You, as the teacher, are the one who sets the tone in the classroom. You can choose to be the kind of teacher who approaches planning, teaching, and student success from a positive perspective. You can make the choice to focus on the positive aspects of your job, including your interactions with students, parents, administrators, and colleagues.

Teachers can build a positive climate in the classroom by setting the stage for positive interactions—praising good performance, incorporating a variety of reward ideas, and, most important, making the students believe in themselves. Once students gain confidence, they will blossom. Focusing on the positive is the key.

There is always something, no matter how small, that you can point out as a positive. Perhaps it is the way a student writes a letter; perhaps it is how the student signs his or her name. Building from a positive experience always elicits a better response.

This doesn't mean that you don't point out your students' mistakes. A teacher must make students aware of their mistakes in order for the students to learn. However, you should plan your delivery so that you note an example of something that the student has done correctly before you point out a mistake. This serves as a reminder to the student that although there is still much to learn, he or she already knows many things and can do them correctly. This delivery also helps the teacher focus on the students' strengths rather than only on the students' weaknesses or problem behavior.

The following are suggestions for building a positive climate in your classroom:

- Communicate expectations clearly to your students.
- Hold high expectations for student work.
- Encourage students to do well.
- Display an encouraging attitude.
- Avoid comparing students to one another.
- For every negative, find a positive.
- Look at mistakes as opportunities.
- Model the idea of "two stars and a wish": For every assignment, find two positive aspects and one you would like to see changed.

A teacher's positive praise creates a strong climate for learning and can be heartening for a student. Students remember the teachers who showed they cared and were positive. You may want to consider the following:

- Be specific with your praise. Instead of just saying, "Good job!" say, "I like the way you started your sentences."
- Determine whether you should praise children publicly (in front of the whole class) or privately (on their papers or quietly during class).
- Use written comments on papers, tests, and other assignments as opportunities for positive praise.
- Write personal notes to your students offering positive praise.
- Use private conversations, conferences with parents, and notes home as opportunities for positive praise.

A positive phone call or conference can have a tremendous impact on a student. Teachers often wait until there is a problem before placing a call home and often don't call at all when there is something positive to share. Try to make a positive call home about each student. This creates a positive environment and may gain the support of parents for a time when you need to place a call home about negative behavior.

Incentives and Rewards

Incentives and rewards provide a mechanism for positive experiences for the students in your classroom, and they add interest and excitement to the classroom routine. A classroom incentive system should have the potential to involve every student in the class. It is important

that an incentive system not limit recognition to only a handful of students. Be mindful not to pass out incentives and rewards too frequently, because they may lose their effectiveness. Most important, always manage incentive systems consistently, and follow through with any awards and rewards.

Recognition

Recognizing students can be a powerful behavior management tool. Recognition teaches students that personal satisfaction is often enough of a reward for making good choices. You can recognize students in many ways.

- Display student work.
- Use certificates of recognition for achievements such as perfect attendance, completed homework, and good citizenship.
- Cite student accomplishments verbally.
- Make a positive phone call home.
- Recognize students at an assembly.
- Post students' names in your room or in the office.
- Photograph recognized students and display the pictures prominently.
- Respond to students' accomplishments in the daily announcements.
- Give students a private smile, wink, or side hug.
- Give students a pat on the back or shoulder.
- Have the entire class give a round of applause to a student.

Privileges

Incentives and rewards don't have to cost money to be effective and meaningful. Giving students a special privilege can be very effective. It may also be easier to follow through with these rewards, because they don't involve a purchase of any sort. Develop an incentive system in which using privileges as rewards works for you—what works in someone else's classroom may not work in yours. Privileges that can be used as rewards might include:

- Free homework pass
- Silent reading time in the library beanbag chairs
- Being appointed the teacher's helper
- Choosing the read-aloud book
- Carrying the stuffed teddy bear for the day
- Sitting in the "teacher's pet" desk
- Using new colored pencils or markers
- Extra recess time
- Lunch with the teacher
- Offering a seat cushion for the day or week

Activities

Offer students an opportunity to participate in special activities as a reward for a job well done. This is a good way to recognize appropriate behavior with no monetary cost to you. It teaches students that good behavior pays off, and it can set an example for students who haven't been recognized yet. Try to give every student a chance to be recognized at some point. Many activities are appropriate to use as rewards for both individual students and the whole class. Suggested activities follow:

- Individual students
  - Free reading time
  - Game time
  - Extra visits to the school library
  - Extra time on the computer
  - Being appointed a special helper
- The whole class
  - Movie on Fridays (Always check school and/or district policies about showing movies during instructional time and for guidelines for acceptable or approved films.)
  - Fifteen minutes of free time at the end of the day or week
  - Game play
  - Listening to approved student-supplied music during art time
  - Free homework night

Tangible Rewards

Tangible rewards are material items such as stickers and school supplies. Many teachers also use food, pencils, erasers, games, toys, and books. Using tangible rewards must be well thought-out for several reasons.

- **Cost**—Items used as tangible rewards are usually an out-of-pocket expense. The rewards used should be consistent throughout the school year, so think about the commitment to certain incentives and their potential cost to you.

- **School/District policy**—Check school and/or district policies related to rewarding students with items, especially food.

- **Student expectations**—It is important to teach students the value of intrinsic incentives as opposed to extrinsic incentives. An incentive system should be structured to help students value a job well done, rather than simply become dependent on tangible rewards.

- **Teacher dependency**—It can be easy for teachers to begin using tangible rewards too much: You get an immediate and positive response from a student who has just been given a sticker or other item. If you choose to use a tangible reward system, use it with discretion and sporadically, so that students can't anticipate a reward. One exception could be using tangible rewards as part of a set routine (for example, during transitions, before lunch, or at the end of the day). Otherwise, it's best to use tangible rewards as one part of a broader incentive system.

If you use tangible rewards as part of your classroom incentive system, remember that what makes an incentive powerful is not so much the item itself as the recognition that comes with it. There are many types of tangible rewards that can be given to individual students or to the whole class.

- Individual students
  - Stickers, stamps, and stars
  - Pencils, erasers, and notepads
  - Prizes, such as small toys, rings, and figurines (available from vendors like Oriental Trading Company)
  - Snacks, such as cookies and Goldfish crackers

- Candy (Use sparingly; be cognizant of food allergies.)
- Certificates
- Tickets (used to shop for a prize at the end of the school week)
- Treasure chest
- Bookmarks
- Books
- Extra credit
- The whole class
    - Popsicle party (monthly)
    - Ice cream party (monthly)
    - Friday popcorn party
    - New book for the library
    - Watching a movie at lunch
    - Points for a reward
    - New classroom game (board game or computer game)
    - Pizza party (monthly or each semester)

Food as Incentive

Using food items as an incentive can cause serious problems, especially where younger students are concerned. Although older students likely know what they can and cannot have, younger students don't always know or remember this. Generally, an allergy or food issue is noted in the student's cumulative record. It is also a good idea to ask parents about their child's allergies in an initial welcome letter (which should always be pre-approved by the school administration). Keep the following considerations in mind if you use food as an incentive.

Allergies, Especially to Nuts You might be surprised to learn that the ingredients of many food items contain some form of nut. This can be extremely dangerous—even to the touch—for a student who has allergies.

Too Much Sugar Parents may have limitations on candy and sugar intake due to medical issues or personal philosophies.

Non-Vegetarian Items Students may come from vegetarian or vegan households.

Religious Restrictions Students may come from families whose religion has restrictions on specific foods (for example, dairy or meat).

Cautions About Using Rewards

When students are rewarded for good behavior or a job well done, they take notice. However, incentives and rewards must be handled well in order to be effective. It is extremely important to put a lot of thought into the incentive system for the students in your class.

For example, if the teacher's objective is to control student behavior through prizes or other extrinsic rewards, students may learn only to comply with specific standards. However, if the teacher's objective is for the students to develop a sense of self-control, tangible rewards should be used only sparingly, so that students learn the value of a job well done for its own sake.

- Avoid rewards given to control or shape behavior.
- Give positive feedback for student competence in place of tangible rewards.
- Be consistent, and always follow through with the rewards that have been earned. This is a matter of trust between you and your students, and you never want to break that trust.
- Avoid giving rewards all day, all the time.

Managing Misbehavior

Certain inappropriate behaviors need to be addressed immediately so that students don't continue them. Such behaviors include lack of participation, inattention, avoidance of work, and violation of classroom rules and procedures. All of these behaviors should be dealt with directly, but without overreacting. A calm approach is the most productive way to handle such behaviors. Some tactics to consider are the following:

- **"The Look"**—Make eye contact with or stare at a student to show that you mean business.
- **Proximity**—Move closer to the student while you continue to teach.
- **A signal**—Use a signal, such as a finger to the lips or a shake of the head, to correct misbehavior.
- **A reminder**—Remind a student of the correct rules.
- **Redirection**—When a student is off task, redirect his or her attention to the task: "Jackson, let's get working on those math facts. It's almost time for lunch." or "I like the way Maria is working on her math facts."

- **A conference**—Quietly tell the student to stop the inappropriate behavior. This can be handled within the class but with a lowered voice, so that other students are not able to hear what you said.

When a student continues to demonstrate unacceptable behavior, other alternatives should be considered.

- Talk briefly with the student at recess or lunch.
- Give the student a time-out at a desk or chair away from the group or activity.
- Send the child to another teacher's classroom to complete the assignment. The student should go with a specific task to work on and only for a short period of time. Know your school or district policy on this.

Misbehavior in the Classroom

When students misbehave in class, it interferes with teaching, stifles learning, produces stress, and leads to poor class morale. It may upset both the teacher and the other students. Managing inappropriate behavior in class is one of the most difficult things that a teacher has to deal with in the classroom.

Just as creating a positive classroom environment lessens the need for discipline, it is important to handle misbehavior in a positive manner rather than a negative one.

Keep in mind that it is the misbehavior, not the student, that you have issues with. It is important to differentiate the two for the student: "Johnny, I don't dislike you. I dislike your behavior and the choices you are making." Let students know that you like all of them as individuals, but that you have issues with some of their behavior choices. Inappropriate behavior leads to specific consequences, and when a student misbehaves, you are required to follow the guidelines that govern the classroom.

When your students misbehave, don't take it personally. There are many factors that can result in students' acting out. There may be emotional or physiological factors that are beyond a student's control. Knowing this may help you better understand why a student is acting out. It is not your job to diagnose your students or to conduct a social work investigation. However, be aware, and report any concerns to the appropriate authority.

Identifying Misbehavior

Appropriate classroom behavior is demonstrated when students are responsible, have self-control, and respect one another.

Misbehavior in the classroom is any behavior that interferes with teaching or learning. This includes any action that is inappropriate for the setting (classroom, auditorium, gymnasium) or situation (during a lesson, on the playground, at the lunch tables) in which it occurs.

Types of Misbehavior

- Inattention
- Lack of participation
- Talking too much in class
- Lack of respect for authority
- Getting out of one's seat needlessly
- Distracting or disrupting others
- Lying
- Stealing
- Cheating
- Sexual harassment
- Fighting
- Bullying
- Vandalism

Discipline and Flexibility

In order to manage a classroom successfully, every teacher must have an established discipline plan to handle student misbehavior. Discipline is an integral part of teaching. Your classroom has a protocol of established rules, consequences, and procedures, and these should be followed to facilitate learning.

Discipline and punishment are two different things, however. Punishment is often expressed with anger or raising one's voice, both of which can be counterproductive. Discipline often requires you to be flexible, letting go of some of the little things so you can successfully handle the bigger ones. A discipline plan must include dealing with behavior that is clearly unacceptable and is interfering with classroom instruction. It is important to realize, however, that if you tried to discipline every instance of misbehavior, you'd never get to your actual teaching. Consider the following:

- Build a relationship with your students, and they will want to work with you.
- Be personable.
- Tell a quick story to help students relate to you.
- Realize that as an adult, you have more life experience.
- Avoid a no-win situation.
- Avoid situations where misbehaviors happen in close succession, resulting in your losing the whole class.
- Never sound whiny or plead with your students.
- Get inside your students' heads. In time, you will develop an arsenal of strategies to use with students.
- Observe other teachers and ask how they handle certain behaviors; incorporate what works for you.

Converting Inappropriate Behavior

Your behavior management style should include productive ways of working with your students. There are many ways to do this, because everything you do can potentially impact behavior management in your classroom. Fighting a certain behavior constantly may just make it worse—sometimes you just need to go with it. For example, if a student is talkative, have that student take attendance. If a student is fidgety, have that student organize the library or sharpen pencils. You can turn a student's inappropriate behavior into a productive activity. Consider the following:

- Maintain a sense of focus.
- Treat all students equally.
- Know your students' needs and interests.
- Build strong connections with your students.
- Involve students in decision making.
- Know what causes the misbehavior in your student.
- Establish ways to respond directly to specific misbehavior.
- Build trust through consistency.
- Involve parents and guardians as much as possible.

Techniques for Managing Behavior

There are numerous techniques you can employ in your classroom to manage behavior.

- **Nonverbal cues**—Use a head shake or a finger to the lips.
- **Moving the activity along**—Maintain smooth transitions and appropriate pacing.
- **Proximity**—Circulate as you teach.
- **Group focus**—Use a system of table points and hold the whole group accountable.
- **Behavior redirection**—Note that other students or groups are doing what they should be doing.
- **Needed instruction**—Work with small groups of struggling students and preteach and/or reteach them.
- **A brief halt**—Tell the student to stop the undesirable behavior. Make direct eye contact and be assertive.
- **Offering a choice**—Advise the misbehaving student to either stop the offending behavior and move on, or continue the misbehavior with a consequence.
- **Withholding a privilege**—Withhold an appropriate privilege for the specific misbehavior.
- **Isolation or removal of students**—Send a student to another teacher's classroom to complete an assignment.
- **Detention at recess or lunch**—Assign detention for an appropriate length of time for the specific misbehavior.
- **Referral to the school office**—Use this option as a last resort.

Anecdotal Records

If a student's particular misbehavior is either consistent or severe enough, you must document it fully—everything from the actual behavior to the details of your handling of it. It is important to keep your notes in a designated folder for use when conferencing with parents, the administration, or the student. This is especially important when misbehavior results in the need for an incident report or a problem-solving intervention. Check with the school for appropriate policy and procedures concerning behavior documentation and referral.

01
Anecdotal Log
17
Incident Reports

When documenting an incident of misbehavior, refer to your anecdotal records. The **Anecdotal Log** and **Incident Reports** templates can be used for this purpose.

- **Time and date**—When did the misbehavior occur?
- **Location**—Where did it take place?
- **Incident**—What did the student do? What happened?
- **Witnesses**—Who was present?
- **Initial response**—What did you do? What was done?
- **Follow-up**—How did you follow up? With whom? (for example, the office, referral, home communication)
- **Follow-up feedback/Action plan**—What will be done in the long term?

Addressing Concerns About Behavior

In most cases, communicating expectations clearly and taking action promptly are effective in addressing concerns about behavior. However, every student is unique, so certain strategies may work better with some students than with others. Here are some suggestions:

- **A talk**—Try to find time to talk to the student. Get to know the student and connect with him or her. This establishes trust and makes it harder for the student to act out. Remember that you should never meet alone with a student. Keep the door open, preferably with other students in the classroom, when meeting with a student.
- **Ignoring the problem**—If a behavior problem is ignored, it may intensify and spread to other students. Consider having students work out their conflicts with one another. This helps them take responsibility for their behavior. The **Conflict Resolution Slips** template can be used for this purpose.
- **Referral to the office**—Referring a student to the office takes little of the teacher's time, but it doesn't necessarily deal with the behavior problem in the classroom. It may even give a student the upper hand, since the student may perceive that you were unable to handle the problem in the classroom.
- **A call home**—Calling the parents may work, but parents can't always help with misbehavior in the classroom. If you do call home, try to find something positive to report, too. In any case, follow up quickly with a positive call home once the student's behavior improves. This can establish a trusting rapport with the parents, which can be very helpful.
- **Consequences**—Administering punishment as a consequence for inappropriate behavior may stop the behavior temporarily and deter others, though it could also cause resentment. Punishment alone, however, does little to teach the student self-control and responsibility.

10
Conflict
Resolution
Slips

Each of these strategies has its limitations, so you'll want to incorporate multiple means of addressing misbehavior.

It is possible to overreact to a situation when caught up in the moment. New teachers, especially, may overreact, assuming the worst. After a bit of time has passed, the infraction may not seem quite as bad. Establishing a flexible protocol can help eliminate this problem. Follow protocol, but know that there are times when flexibility is called for. Put yourself in the student's place: Would your reaction and handling of the situation seem fair?

Sometimes, misbehavior stems from problems that a student is dealing with outside the classroom as well as inside it. Knowing about these problems can help you communicate with the student.

Outside Problems

- Lack of sleep
- Shuffling between two homes because of divorced parents
- An inadequate breakfast
- Poor nutrition
- An argument with a sibling or parent before coming to school
- Lack of a quiet place to study
- Living in an abusive home situation
- Problems on the playground with classmates or other school peers
- Too much time spent in extracurricular activities and not enough time dedicated to schoolwork

Give a student the benefit of the doubt whenever you can. Empathy on your part can go a long way. You may be the only person who recognizes the good in that student. In certain situations, you may be all a particular student has.

Inside Problems

- Not enough exposure to, or background experience with, the curriculum
- Insufficient English language ability
- Low level of subject-specific mastery
- Lack of materials and books
- Lack of support for new or difficult concepts
- Diagnosed special needs and benchmarks that are not being considered when instruction is planned and delivered
- Misunderstanding or disregard for the student's learning styles and interests by the teacher

Meeting the Students' Needs

Whether a student's problems originate inside the classroom or outside of it, the teacher must evaluate the situation and make every effort to meet the student's needs within the classroom. Oftentimes, when we find approaches or tactics that are helpful in engaging students, our students are more likely to participate, and this minimizes the time when misbehavior can occur.

However, sometimes a situation with a student doesn't resolve so easily. In these cases, it is important to remember your role in the process. You are an educator, and your job is to educate the students who arrive in your classroom with many different needs. As teacher, you have to meet those needs, possibly by exhausting all options for modified instruction.

If you think a student may need a referral for support beyond what you are able to provide, observe and take notes. A student's needs may, in fact, be beyond your expertise. Refer students to other professionals as needed, and remember that referral is not passing the buck—it is about meeting the needs of the student. Referrals are typically reviewed and require documentation showing that the teacher has tried a series of modifications and strategies first. Check with your school to learn about the referral process.

Communicating with Parents

A basic component of teaching is communicating with parents. (Keep in mind that this category might include parents, a relative, or an appointed guardian.) Although a student's misbehavior may require a parent-teacher conference, this meeting should not be the first time a parent learns about concerns with behavior or grades. In order to avoid potential problems, consider the following:

- Contact parents regularly (within reason) about a student's behavior problem before it is necessary to conference with them.
- Offer several choices for a meeting time—before school, after school, or even by phone.
- Have documentation about the child's pattern of behavior available to refer to during the conference. This documentation can be in the form of anecdotal notes, weekly progress reports, referral notices, a log of phone calls home, or interventions by another teacher or an administrator. The **Anecdotal Log** and **Weekly Progress Reports** templates can be used for this purpose.

01
Anecdotal
Log
49
Weekly
Progress
Reports

- Call the parents by name, using a title (Mr., Mrs., Ms., Dr.) and their last name unless you are told to use their first names.
- Greet the parents warmly. Begin the conversation with something positive about the student before discussing the student's behavior issues.
- Have the parents sit with you at a table where adult-sized chairs are available. It is best to be at the same level when talking about their child.
- Consider the parents' feelings throughout the conference. You don't know everything about the situation at home.
- Maintain eye contact. If you need to refer to a note or folder, tell them that you are going to look something up so they don't think you are ignoring them in any way.
- State simply and clearly why they are there. Give a few specific examples. Stay focused on key issues.
- Keep the conversation on track. Don't let it digress into personal issues. The student and his or her behavior in school are the sole reason for the conference.
- Listen attentively when parents share their perspective. Wait until they complete their thoughts before you speak. Keep a notepad handy for jotting down a topic to discuss so you're not tempted to interrupt them.
- Ask the parents for their input. What are they doing at home to meet their child's behavioral and academic needs that might help you at school? What did last year's teacher do to support their child that they thought was productive?
- Do not discuss other students. If the parent tries to shift the blame to other students, stay focused on their child. Avoid comparing their child to other students.
- Focus on the classroom rules, consequences, and procedures. Discuss the consequences for not demonstrating appropriate behavior.
- Consider giving parents some concrete ideas for behavior management at home. You may want to create a behavior contract if the situation calls for one.
- After the conference, document what was discussed.

5 Getting Off to a Good Start

How you manage the first few days of the new school year with your students can set the stage for the entire year. Students are often on their best behavior at this point, because they still need to get to know you, your classroom policies, and each other. You can take advantage of this by being prepared with a well thought-out classroom management system. While it's certainly possible to reestablish control or try new strategies during the year, it's important to establish good patterns in the classroom from the very first day. Key to this is establishing a strong community of learners who know and trust one another, and who are motivated to learn from you. You can facilitate this by helping your students get to know one another. In this chapter, you will find several "get to know you" activities for the first few days of school.

Teaching Routines and Procedures

You must communicate your expectations about appropriate student behavior to your students from the minute the students enter your classroom. Your first couple of weeks should be spent putting your students through a "boot camp" experience, where they learn and practice the classroom routines and procedures that have been established. This is especially important in the primary grades, where it takes more time for students to learn what a typical day in your classroom involves. While an intensive "boot camp" experience takes valuable time, it may ultimately save time by creating an efficient, well-managed classroom. There are several different ways to accomplish this.

Describing and Modeling Desired Behavior

When communicating your expectations about appropriate student behavior, be specific about how you want students to do things—not only inside the classroom, but also anywhere on the school campus. Model appropriate behavior for your students. You might incorporate role-play opportunities for given scenarios to see how they would respond to specific situations. Allow opportunities for problem solving by your students. They may very well come up with a better way to handle a classroom procedure. You can then add this to your list of routine ways to do things and refer to it when needed. Possible scenarios to role-play include the following:

- Lining up for a fire drill or emergency
- Entering the classroom at the beginning of the day, taking out homework, and storing backpacks
- Visiting the library and checking out books
- Entering the cafeteria, sitting at assigned tables, eating lunch, discarding trash, and exiting to the playground

Students Respond to Appropriate Classroom Routines

In addition to role-playing, for which you create a scenario, you can ask open-ended questions. Ask your students to share—either in writing or verbally—how they would approach a specific task. This activity allows students to demonstrate their understanding, and it shows that you have been clear in your expectations. Possibilities include what they should do during the following classroom activities:

- Sharpening pencils
- Obtaining materials or supplies, such as paper, Kleenex, or a book
- Asking for help
- Answering a question
- Talking to a neighbor
- Finishing a task or activity early
- Going to the restroom

Give Appropriate Feedback

It's important for students to know when they are following classroom rules and procedures properly and when they are not. Consider reviewing the following procedures and routines with your students:

- Entering and exiting the classroom (at recess, lunch, and the end of the day)
- Storing coats and backpacks
- Collecting and distributing homework
- Moving around the classroom (to the rug area, to centers, and to small group areas)
- Distributing materials and supplies (such as paper, scissors, and glue)
- Sharpening pencils and exchanging broken pencils for new ones
- Using games and puzzles
- Cleaning up
- The morning routine, such as the calendar and attendance
- Daily routines, such as "Do Now" activities, journals, and silent reading

All students, especially younger students, need structure and routine in the classroom. By the time students get to the third or fourth grade, they have begun to develop a better sense of school culture and procedures. Think through your classroom procedures. How do you want things to be done? As you move through a typical day, jot down notes about procedures that aren't working so you can ask other teachers how they handle the same procedure. Take the opportunity to observe other teachers or ask them how they handle daily routines, such as passing out papers or referring students to the office who have misbehaved. See Chapter 3, Establishing Rules, Consequences, and Procedures.

Creating a Congenial and Positive Climate in Your Classroom

Design a strong classroom management plan before the school year starts, but make part of it the creation of a congenial, positive classroom environment— a welcoming space where learning occurs comfortably. This climate should be in place on the very first day of school. Teachers joke about not smiling until after Christmas—maintaining a strong and professional teacher stance in order to establish oneself and earn students' respect. This can all be done within a congenial and positive climate.

A positive environment encourages students to be excited about coming to school every day and excited about learning. A congenial environment allows your students to be comfortable with you and at the same time to respect you as their teacher. It lets the students know that you genuinely want them in your classroom. Creating this kind of classroom environment involves meaningful interactions between the teacher and students and also among the students themselves. Students spend most of their waking hours with their teachers. It's important to create a sense of belonging in your classroom, especially at the beginning. Don't make students wait until after the winter holiday—three or four months into the school year— before they feel that they belong in your classroom. Consider these ways to create a congenial and positive environment in your classroom:

- **Speak calmly and politely.** Students should hear teachers say "please" and "thank you." Share information; learn about your students and share some of your life with them.
- **Use positive reinforcement.** Comment on positive behavior and give immediate, specific feedback for a job well done.
- **Establish a feeling of community.** Have students help set up some of the bulletin boards with their own pictures, work, and ideas.
- **Keep your voice at a moderate level.** Try not to raise your voice when you need to get students' attention. Keep your voice at a quiet, even level, and your students will too.

Teacher Authority

The concept of teacher authority encompasses your right to set standards for student behavior and performance. You must always keep in mind that you are your students' teacher, not their friend. You may very well be the only authority figure in the lives of some of your students— the only person who sets boundaries and has high expectations for them. Take this role seriously. Students need you to preserve the boundary that sets you apart from them. Be "friendly" without trying to be their friend. You may be their cheerleader, their rule-setter, their disciplinarian, their counselor, and their confidant, but their friends need to be their own age.

Classroom management theorists such as Lee and Marlene Canter describe three types of teachers: hostile, nonassertive, and assertive (see Chapter 1, Theorists). What kind of teacher do you want to be? Consider the attributes of an assertive teacher:

- Provides reasons for rules and avoids using threats and punishment to control students
- Maintains a democratic classroom instead of one where the teacher is completely in charge
- Administers consequences fairly and consistently, and avoids assigning consequences arbitrarily without student input
- Explains the basis for the teacher's actions and decisions
- Gives students more independence as they demonstrate more maturity

Rules and Consequences

The discussion of classroom rules and consequences should be a democratic experience, where students have some input regarding the consequences for classroom rules. School rules, and the consequences associated with them, should be discussed together with your classroom rules. You may want to test students on the rules and consequences, or you may have them write out the rules and have their parents sign them. Post the rules in the classroom as a reminder for students.

The First Days of the School Year

The first days of the school year are critical for many reasons. There is a lot to do and a lot to cover with your students. It could be overwhelming, but you will be able to navigate these early days of the school year successfully if you are prepared for them. Make a list of the general areas you want to cover during the first few days of school. Remind yourself to be patient, because some students will need more time than others to grasp what is expected of them. Cultural background, linguistic level, ability level, and behavior needs all play a part in how quickly some children

show their understanding of these expectations. This may differ from student to student and from year to year. Give your students time to get used to their new classroom, their classmates, and their teacher. Make use of direct instruction and repeated experiences to help your students understand your expectations. Take this time to orient your students in the following areas:

- Expectations
  - Establish expectations as soon as students enter the classroom.
  - Be assertive and clear.
  - Cover areas such as grades, behavior, and attendance.
- Routines
  - Share the class schedule with students.
  - Walk students through the main classroom routines.
  - Model routines physically, and explain them.

- Procedures
  - Model procedures, and have students practice them.
  - Consider the procedures outlined in Teaching Routines and Procedures (page 104).
- Rules
  - Have rules in place for the first day of class.
  - Discuss the importance of rules.
  - Establish new rules as a class, using your own ideas as a launching pad for discussion.

- Consequences
  - Have consequences in place for the first day of class.
  - Share your system for tracking student behavior.
  - Establish new consequences as a class, using your own ideas as a launching pad for discussion.
- Room layout
  - Give a tour of your classroom.
  - Walk around the classroom, explaining the different areas and their purposes.
  - Practice traffic patterns for entering, exiting, and transitioning.

- Curriculum
  - Share an overview of content standards.
  - Distribute student materials during specific curriculum times.
  - Share expectations with regard to caring for textbooks.
  - Share your policy for lost books.
- School policy
  - Review school guidelines (for example, attendance, absences, leaving school).

First Day Tips

- **Mix it up.** Plan a variety of activities that provide movement, short breaks, and a change of pace to help maintain alertness and interest.

- **Sign.** Have a sign with your name and room number on your classroom door. If you are picking up students at a designated location, wear or carry a sign with this information. This helps students and parents find you. Have your class roster with you, so you can check students in who are lining up with you or entering your classroom.

- **Greet.** Greet your students as they enter the classroom. Prepare name tags for students to wear (stickers are best) or have name tags attached to student desks. This is especially important for primary students. Keep in mind that your roster may change, so be flexible and have extra name tags on hand. The **Desk Name Tag** template can be used for this purpose.

12
Desk Name
Tag

- **Share.** Tell students some personal things about yourself. Keep it simple. Then ask students to introduce themselves. Be aware that if you have students tell something about themselves, it could take a lot of time. Monitor the time so that everyone has a chance.

- **Break the ice.** Implement get-acquainted activities, such as those described below and in the section The First Week of School (page 117).

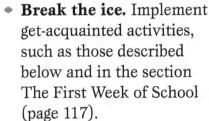

  - Have students introduce themselves to neighbors by telling something interesting about themselves. The neighbor then introduces the rest of the class to the student. The **Student Interest Survey** template can be used for this purpose.

40
Student
Interest Survey

  - Have students introduce themselves by attaching their names to games or adjectives, like "Monopoly Mike," "iPod Isaac," or "Silly Suzanne."
  - Have students complete a brief questionnaire that identifies their interests, subjects, and hobbies.
  - Hold a scavenger hunt where students "hunt" for a student in the class who matches a specific description. The **Scavenger Hunt Questionnaire** template can be used for this purpose.

27
Scavenger
Hunt
Questionnaire

  - Have students write letters about what they hope to learn this year.
  - Have each student bring a brown paper bag containing three to five items they can share about themselves.

Communicating with Families

A vital part of building a relationship with your students is to connect with the parents and families in ways that involve them in their children's schooling. Parent involvement has long been recognized as a positive factor in children's academic and social growth.

Teachers need to establish formal communication with students' homes, such as a letter that contains essential information not already covered in school handouts. Consider including the following points in a "Welcome Back" newsletter:

- Materials and supplies the student will need
  - Check school policy regarding requests for materials.
- Statements about school policy, achievement, and progress
- School contact information
  - Provide the school phone number.
  - Provide your professional e-mail address.
  - Do not provide personal contact information.
- Curriculum units you will be teaching
  - Summarize what you will cover this year.
  - Provide information about state standards.
- School events during the academic year
  - Check the school calendar.
  - Always get approval from the administration for specific dates for events.
  - Include formal meetings, such as conferences.
- Homework information
  - Consult with fellow teachers on their policies.
  - Outline your homework policy.
  - State the consequences for failure to turn in homework.
- Invitations for classroom volunteers
  - Check school policy regarding volunteers.
  - Make sure volunteers know to check in.
- Breakfast and lunch programs
  - Explain program options.
  - Provide financial assistance applications.

Letter Tips

- Your letter should be cheerful and friendly.
- Be sure there are no grammatical errors, misspellings, or typos.
- If possible, provide a translation for families who would benefit from having it in a language other than English.
- Always obtain approval from the office, as with any communication home.
- Include information to let families know how to contact you. Use the school's phone number and your professional (not personal) e-mail address.

Additional Communication Strategies

- Encourage classroom visits.
- Engage in brief conversations with parents during school programs and events.
- Make phone calls home.
- Encourage communication via written notes or e-mail.
- Plan informal home visits, if you think they would be helpful (and if they would be safe).
- Construct an up-to-date class website.

Anticipating Problems

Veteran teachers and new teachers alike have concerns related to classroom management and how to discipline students for inappropriate behavior. If you think ahead and anticipate problems, you can avoid a great many of them. From the very first day, you must communicate clearly to your students what your expectations are and what the consequences will be for not meeting them. There are many basic strategies that can help you anticipate—and avoid—problems in the classroom. Consider the following:

- Avoid being too severe or serious. At the same time, avoid being way too much fun and not serious enough. Find a happy medium. An assertive teacher finds this balance.

- Maintain positive beginnings and endings for lessons and activities. Avoid starting a new activity before gaining the students' attention. This avoids having to repeat yourself or change direction too often. You may want to randomly call on two or three students (table or class leaders for the week, perhaps) to repeat what the class will be working on next. You might post an agenda and time limit for each activity; this can be checked off during the day as activities are completed.

- Intervene as soon as you observe inappropriate student behavior to show that you take the rules seriously. How you apply a consequence is just as important. If a rule is broken, a warning or consequence must be implemented immediately so students understand that you will be fair and consistent with all students.

- Know the difference between reward and acknowledgment, and use each appropriately. It is a good idea to reward students' appropriate behavior, but sometimes a teacher needs only to give a thumbs-up or perhaps give a table point quietly in order to acknowledge a job well done. Constantly using rewards  may encourage students to complete activities only when a reward will be given. If you want students to be on task and act appropriately, the simpler the positive reinforcement, the better. After all, following the rules and turning in homework are part of a student's job. Rewards are best reserved for a meaningful response, helping a classmate, or extra credit.

- Learn students' names and use them consistently within the first week. Take the time to learn how to pronounce each student's given name properly; this shows a sense of welcoming and acceptance. Find out what each student likes to be called. Some students prefer to use a nickname rather than their given name, or a student may choose a more common name to use at school instead of a given name. Use whatever name makes the student most comfortable.

- Require students to use a signal (such as raising their hand) and be acknowledged before they give a response to a question or prompt. Use a system that allows students to share out at appropriate times and that offers a chance for everyone to participate. Hand signs and color cards work well.

- Don't use the same teaching strategy or combination of strategies day after day. Consider different learning styles and Gardner's Multiple Intelligences when planning lessons and delivering instruction. Keep in mind the needs of all of the students in your classroom—traditional students, advanced learners, English language learners, students with special needs, and students from different cultural backgrounds—so that your lessons reflect a variety of approaches. Know your students' interests, and tap into them when you are making a point or giving examples.

- Complete daily and long-range planning so that you are well prepared before you introduce curricular units and teach the individual lessons. Students will know if you are not prepared. Enhance your planning by getting to know the teacher's editions, talking with your grade-level team, and meeting with the curriculum resource administrator if your school has one.

- Don't interrupt students while they are on task. This disrupts their momentum and can easily get them off track. If students are working quietly in small groups or individually, don't interrupt the class as a whole to make a point or to reteach something. Instead, check in with individual students or small groups, especially those that typically need more assistance.

- Don't spend too much time with one student or group. Check in with every student at least three times a day, even if only for 10 or 20 seconds, to monitor independent practice and/or group work.

- Move around the classroom, forcing students' eyes and ears to follow you; don't stand too long in one place. By moving around, you keep students awake and engaged. Avoid sitting too long as well. Effective teachers rarely have time to sit; when they do, it is usually when they are working with individual students or small groups.

- Don't spend a lot of time giving directions for an activity—students may get lost before they get started. Post directions for students who need to refer to them. If possible, include pictures of required steps for the benefit of visual learners and English language learners. You may want to have two or three students in different parts of the classroom repeat the steps back to you, so that everyone hears the directions several times.

- Pace students' activities. You (and therefore your students) can get behind quickly if you dwell too long on a single activity, which may cause you to play catch-up for the rest of the day or week. Use a kitchen or digital timer to help you stay on track. You may be able to put a student helper in charge of the timer.

- Pay attention to your delivery. Don't talk too fast, or you may well lose several of your students. You are very likely to have English language learners, students with special needs, and/or struggling students in your class. Stop periodically and review, or have a student summarize what you have said.

41
Student
Name Cards
42
Student
Name Strips

- Make sure that each student gets a turn. Don't fall into the trap of calling on only the smartest students or only those who always have their hand raised. Use a system for randomly calling names, such as having all your students' names on cards, Popsicle sticks, or poker chips and picking one at random until each name has been called. The **Student Name Cards** and **Student Name Strips** templates can be used for this purpose. If you use a SMART Board, you can type students' names into the Random Word Generator Notebook and use this program to randomly select students' names. Selecting students randomly keeps them all on their toes and ready to respond when called on. It also allows equal treatment of boys and girls, students of different ability levels, and so on.

- Don't overuse verbal techniques to stop inappropriate student behavior. If you try to talk over classroom noise, it just gets louder. Avoid using "shhh" to try to quiet students. Instead, use a variety of techniques to quiet the class, such as a hand signal, a repeatable clap, a countdown, body gestures, a fun bell, or a timer.

- Use a voice level that makes students lean in and listen but isn't so quiet that they can't hear you. Reserve speaking at your highest volume for times when you need to get your students' attention in an emergency.

- Don't use threats to control the class. Threats work only rarely, and when they do, it's usually for only a brief period of time.

- Never reprimand a student in front of the class. This ridicules and embarrasses the student in front of his or her peers, and it damages the trust that you have built with your class. It may cause students to fear you or be afraid to participate in class, neither of which is a goal of teaching.

You can no doubt think of other problems on your own. Approach them with care and thought. Take your time assessing situations, and then respond. There may be moments you wish you could do over, but responding thoughtfully can keep those times to a minimum.

The First Week of School

From the first moment that students and their parents set foot in your classroom, you may want to jump right in and explain policies and procedures, rules and consequences, expectations for the school year, and so forth. These are important, but it is at least as important to get to know your students. In order for you to plan and deliver instruction to a new class, you must know them, know where they come from, and know what interests them. They must also have a chance to get to know one another. The following activities offer opportunities to do just that. Remember to model any activity. This will give them a chance to know you, too.

Four-Corner Name Tag (Grades 2-6)

Creating Four-Corner Name Tags helps students get to know one another and helps you get to know their interests and backgrounds. Have each student fold a sheet of 8½″ × 11″ paper into a three-fold tent. In the middle section, the student writes his or her name large enough to fill the space and be seen by you from your desk. In the four corners of the name tag, the student draws or writes four different ways to be identified. The **Desk Name Tag** template can be used for this purpose. A student named Maria might create a Four-Corner Name Tag as described here:

12
Desk Name
Tag

- She writes "Maria" in the center of the middle section of the name tag.
- In one corner, she may draw a book or write "reader."
- In the second corner, she may draw a swimming pool or write "swimmer."
- In the third corner, she may draw herself or write "daughter."
- In the fourth corner, she may draw an Italian flag or write "Italian."

As a warm-up, students can share their name tags in groups of four to six, then take turns sharing with the whole class.

"I Come From" Poem (Grades 3-6)

This activity helps you become acquainted with each student's background and family life. Use the **"I Come From" Poem Planner** template, and encourage rich detail. Be sure to share yours as a model. Descriptions include the following:

16
"I Come From" Poem Planner

- A time in your childhood when you felt the happiest
- A time or place in your childhood when/where you felt the safest
- A time with a sibling, cousin, or other family member that made you laugh really hard, and only the two of you understood why you were laughing
- The place where you grew up (the city, your house, your street)
- Your favorite season and why you love it
- Your favorite food
- A time when you were sad, scared, or confused
- A day that was so perfect you couldn't possibly imagine anything better
- Your favorite holiday or celebration spent with your family

15
"I Am" Poem Planner

You might also use the **"I Am" Poem Planner** template to help students describe themselves.

Once the poem planners have been completed, students write their poems, perhaps with a cover page illustration. Students share their poems in groups of four to six, then with the whole class. You may want to post the poems with cover pages on a Back to School Night bulletin board.

Cultural Symbols (Grades 4-6)

In this activity, each student illustrates a symbol that represents who he or she is as an individual and then explains it to the class. Guide students in understanding that this symbol can reflect who they are in terms of their culture, their family, or their generation. Remind them that culture is not only about ethnicity and race. Suggestions for this activity include the following:

- Illustrate and describe the significance of the flag of their family's country of origin.
- Draw a picture of a computer or gaming system that represents their generation.
- Draw and describe a religious symbol.
- Draw and describe a favorite sport or other activity.

Students share their cultural symbols in groups of four to six, then with the whole class. You may want to post the illustrations on a Back to School Night bulletin board.

Map the School (Grades K–3)

This activity familiarizes students with the school building and is especially valuable for those who are new to the school.

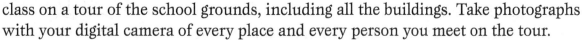

On the first day of school, after reviewing general policies and procedures, take your class on a tour of the school grounds, including all the buildings. Take photographs with your digital camera of every place and every person you meet on the tour.

- Start out by visiting the office to meet the office staff and the principal and vice-principal, if possible.
- Visit the library.
- Visit the computer lab.
- Visit the cafeteria.
- Visit the playground.
- Visit the restrooms.
- Visit the auditorium.
- Visit the gym.
- Visit other areas that students may have access to, for example, the bus drop-off or the garden.

When you return to your classroom, have students work in small groups to create a large scaled drawing of the school, writing the names of the people and places they visited on the appropriate places on the map. Before the end of the day, print the photographs you took.

The following day, ask students to place the photographs in the appropriate places on the map of the school. Have them label each photograph, including the names of teachers, the principal, and other school personnel, as well as the names of the areas visited, such as classrooms, cafeteria, and library. Keep the map posted in the classroom for the first few weeks of school, until students have a good idea of where everything is located.

Name Signs: Who Am I? (Grades 2–6)

This variation of Four-Corner Name Tag helps students learn about one another's interests, likes, and dislikes. It can help you connect with your students, and it can help them begin to build relationships with one another based on similarities.

- Distribute 8½″ × 11″ sheets of paper.
- Ask students to write their names in large colorful letters in the middle of the page.
- In the top left corner, have students finish the sentence "My family and friends think I am _____."
- In the top right corner, have students finish the sentence "My favorite activity is _____."
- In the bottom left corner, have students finish the sentence "I really don't enjoy _____."
- In the bottom right corner, have students finish the sentence "I really enjoy _____."
- In the top center, have students finish the sentence "One day I want to travel to _____."
- In the bottom center, have students finish the sentence "I'd like to meet _____."

Have students share their name signs in groups of four, then with the whole class. You may want to have your students place their name signs on their desks to identify their physical space for Back to School Night.

Small Group Venn (Grades 3–6)

A traditional way to show similarities and differences is with a Venn diagram. It might be used, for example, in brainstorming activities to compare and contrast ideas for character development. Venn diagrams can also be used to help students get to know one another.

- Guide students in developing questions such as "Who is your favorite entertainer?" "When is your birthday?" and "What sports or activities do you like?"

- Divide students into pairs or small groups of three or four.
- Give each group a large sheet of light-colored construction or chart paper and a different color of marker for each student.
- Have each group draw a large Venn diagram consisting of overlapping circles, with one circle for each student.
- Encourage students to discover their similarities and differences by referring to the questions you developed as a class. One student in each group records the responses, writing similarities in the overlaps and differences in the outer circles.
- At an outside edge of the diagram, have students list one or two things that they want to learn or are looking forward to in the school year.
- Have students write their names on the sheet outside of the Venn diagram so that others know which color belongs to which student.
- Each group leaves its Venn diagram on the table and, in five-minute rotations, circulates from table to table to read the diagrams of other groups.

Welcome Brochure for Parents (Grades 4-6)

Within the first week of school, after reviewing general policies and procedures, create a class brochure for parents. Brainstorm with students what to include in the brochure. Revisit the policies and procedures discussed earlier in the week, and transcribe students' ideas on the board. Each student then produces a trifold, decorated brochure to take home to his or her parents. The brochure might include the following information:

- A list of rules and consequences
- Upcoming events for the first month of school
- Homework for the next week
- Five goals that the student has set for himself or herself for the year
- The bell schedule
- Ways to contact the office and the teacher
- Information about the teacher that students learned that day

This is an unusual and creative way to give parents a glimpse of the class from their child's point of view.

Name Puzzle (Grades K-6)

- Using a large sheet of poster board (or several sheets lined up together), draw several interlocking puzzle pieces, one for each student in the class and one for you.
- Number each piece by the order in which it will be put back, then cut out all pieces.
- Talk with the class about how the students in the class are like the puzzle: They are all individuals, but when they are put together and work together as a team, they become complete and they are much stronger.
- Give each student a puzzle piece.
- Have each student write his or her name in the center of the puzzle piece and decorate it, perhaps to show a hobby.
- Have students fit their puzzle pieces together on a large table.
- When the puzzle is complete, carefully tape the pieces together and hang the puzzle as classroom art. You may want to laminate it.

Scavenger Hunt (Grades 3-6)

27
Scavenger
Hunt
Questionnaire

In this activity, students find classmates who fit the descriptions on the **Scavenger Hunt Questionnaire** template. Students introduce themselves before asking a question of a person they do not know. When they find someone who matches a description, they write the person's name down next to that description. A person's name can only be used once on a questionnaire. The individual with the most matches wins.

If you create your own list of descriptions, consider the students in your class: Avoid questions that are biased, whether culturally, linguistically, by ability, or by gender.

Students can then introduce fellow students based on attributes, for example, "This is Kimberly and she likes to run."

Time Capsule (Grades 2-6)

In this activity, students create time capsules that are opened at the end of the year. Because this activity takes considerable time, you may need to continue it into the second week of school, but try to finish the project within a couple of weeks' time. The **Time Capsule** template can be used for this purpose.

48
Time Capsule

- Give each student a manila envelope, to be used as a time capsule. The student can decorate the envelope.
- Each student chooses items to include in his or her time capsule. Contents may include the following:
  - A photograph of the student taken on the first day of school
  - A handwriting sample of the student
  - A tracing of the student's hand or foot (for comparison at the end of the year)
  - A piece of yarn measuring the student's height (for comparison at the end of the year). As an alternative, you could record the height of each class member on a sheet of butcher paper, then cut it apart so that each student can include his or her section in the time capsule. You might have students record how many Unifix cubes tall they are.
  - Any item that will indicate growth in nine months' time
  - A self-portrait by the student
  - A letter from the student—about what the student wants to learn, his or her expectations for the school year, or his or her fears for the school year
- Have each student complete an inventory of his or her time capsule.
- Hold a short ceremony, then place the time capsules in a plastic bin or packing box and tape the lid shut. Do not open until the last week of school.

Goals for the Year (Grades 2–6)

In this activity, students set realistic goals for themselves, based on their current grade level. Students can write their own goals. You may also want to have some goals prepared in advance, or you can brainstorm ideas as a whole class.

- As a whole class, brainstorm relevant goals and transcribe these ideas on a graphic organizer or chart paper.
- Have students write letters in which they describe how they feel about being in their current grade. Encourage them to use the brainstorming ideas.
- You may want to post the letters on Back to School Night.

Culture Bag (Grades 3–6)

In this activity, students create a classroom environment where different cultures are recognized and appreciated. Have each student fill a small bag with five to eight items that represent him or her culturally. Be sure to model for the students, using items from your own culture. Cultural items that may be included are the following:

- Photograph of the student's family
- Small flag representing the country of origin of the student's family
- CD of music played while the student was growing up
- CD of the student's favorite music today
- Piece of jewelry representing the student's religious beliefs
- Doll or toy unique to the student's culture
- Photograph or artwork depicting something that the student feels close to
- Article of traditional clothing

For variety, students should include only one item from each category. Make sure that students have received parental permission to bring all items to school.

As a warm-up, students share their culture bags in groups of four to six, then take turns sharing with the whole class. Items could be displayed on a table for everyone to see. Students can share items unique to their family and upbringing if they don't have a distinct cultural background. If you do this activity in the early weeks of the school year, students can display their culture bags on Back to School Night, giving families an opportunity to get to know the students in their child's class.

Who Do You Think I Am? (Grades K-6)

This activity gives you the opportunity to introduce yourself in a fun way, and it makes your students wonder about you. It allows you to share a little information about yourself without standing in front of the classroom and telling students— you can show them. Include ways to show them about your life as a teacher, about  how learning was easy or difficult for you, and about how you hope they learn all they need to know before moving on to the next school year.

- Bring a bag to school that contains items identifying who you are, such as a running shoe, a plant, an award, or a graduation tassel.
- Divide students into groups. Place a few items on each table, and give students a few minutes to decide what they think each item says about you.
- Have students take turns telling what an item is and what this says about you. Don't disagree with a student until everyone has spoken about the items.
- Circulate from table to table and explain each item, letting students know what you think it says about you.
- Have students complete a questionnaire that asks where they were born, where they have lived, whom they live with, where they have previously attended school, and what their favorite or least favorite subject is.
- Invite students to bring in two or three of their own items to share the following day.

Classroom Quilt (Grades K-6)

This activity demonstrates each student's uniqueness in terms of culture, family background, interests, and hobbies.

- Give each student a square of cloth (8″ × 8″, 10″ × 10″, or 12″ × 12″).
- Hand out supplies like puff paints, pastels, colored pencils, or crayons. (Make sure the supplies are for use on cloth.)
- Have students decorate the squares with representations of their culture, family, favorite sport, what they want to be when they grow up, and so on. You can brainstorm ideas as a class.
- Be sure that students include their names on the squares.
- After the squares are decorated, they can be sewn together (perhaps by a parent volunteer) to form a curtain, room divider, or wall hanging for the year.

Final Thoughts

Whether you are a new or veteran teacher, the first days of the school year can cause anxiety. Being well prepared and knowing exactly what you want to accomplish are key to getting off to a good start. Keep the following ideas in mind as you plan the first days of school.

- Include students in deciding classroom rules and consequences.
- Practice classroom procedures so that students understand what is expected of them.
- Be assertive and consistent. Set up your rules; model and role-play how each rule applies. Be consistent in applying the consequences right from the start.
- Recognize and praise. As students get used to the rules and procedures of their new classroom, look for positive aspects as well as areas that need improvement.
- Over-prepare. Have plenty of activities ready to use on the first day and to fill downtime during the first week or two while you are assessing the students and getting to know them.
- Don't be afraid to dive into your curriculum, but allow flexibility for team-building and get-to-know-you activities.

Most important, enjoy the first days of school. Get to know your students. Let them get to know you. The stronger the bond you form with your students, the more willing they will be to learn from you and actively participate in learning. These first days are critical in making important connections between you and your students and among the students themselves.

6 Know Your Support Team

Teachers—especially at a new or large school—may find it difficult to know everyone on the faculty and staff and to sort out what roles they play on the school campus. At most schools, this includes a principal, vice-principal, office staff, teachers, curriculum coordinators, counselors, nurses, aides, volunteers, and other support staff. All of these people, together with the parents of your students, serve as a support team for you and your class throughout the school year. When each of these people functions well as part of an effective team, the school can run with efficiency and ease. Students' needs are met, and meaningful and productive education is delivered.

Just as the role of a classroom teacher is well defined, the role played by each of the other people on the support team is, too. When a student's situation requires expertise beyond what you can or should provide, you must know which member of your support team you should turn to. It is therefore imperative for you to know what service or assistance can be provided by the person in each of these roles. You may want to establish a relationship with everyone on your support team well before you need their expertise in a specific situation. This will facilitate their becoming involved when you need their help. In this chapter, you will learn about the different people who are on your support team and what role they play in your teaching life.

Connecting with the Team

Every teacher is different. Some are very outgoing, while others are reserved. Regardless of personality type, all teachers should relate to the school staff, the faculty, and the community in a friendly yet professional manner. Consider the following approaches:

- Introduce yourself and share information about yourself.
- Simply say "hello."
- Stop to visit with someone and ask, "How are you doing?"
- Lend a helping hand.
- Sit next to the person at lunch.
- Walk the person to his or her car.
- Send a card.
- Wish the person a happy birthday.
- Recognize the person on an occasion such as the following, which are school related:
  - Secretary's Day (Administrative Professional's Day)—the last Wednesday in April
  - Administrative Professional's Week—the last week of April

- National Teacher Day—the first Tuesday in May
- Teacher Appreciation Week—the first full week in May
- Lend a listening ear (but be careful not to get involved in someone's personal drama).
- Sit next to the person at a faculty meeting.
- Get involved in the PTA or a parent's group.
- Help at school events and functions.
- Volunteer for a position, for example, on the school's emergency team (but be sure you can devote the time necessary to do a good job).

It only takes a minute or two to make a connection with someone, yet it is an investment that is well worth the time. To maintain a professional relationship with your support team, however, means not getting caught up in school drama. Keep in mind that there is a fine line between making a connection and getting caught up in something that could have your name attached to it on the gossip rounds. Consider the following:

- Avoid gossip in the teacher's lounge and cafeteria.
- Be pleasant with everyone.
- Don't be quick to judge.
- If you have nothing nice to say, don't say anything at all.
- Mind your own business—not other people's business.
- Choose friends wisely.
- Always act professional.
- Adhere to school rules and policies.
- Be on time, even if others aren't.

Members of the Team

Being a team player is important, and each player has a designated job. The following is a look at each of these jobs. Job descriptions will vary, depending on the school or district.

Teachers

General Education Teacher

The general education teacher manages a classroom of students and, in addition, is in charge of planning curriculum for an assigned grade level or subject area. Unlike teachers who are specialists, the general education teacher takes into account the needs of all the students in the classroom—traditional students, English language learners, students with special needs, advanced learners, and students from diverse cultural backgrounds. The role of the general education teacher includes the following:

- Planning the standards-based curriculum for a grade level or subject area
- Working collaboratively with other grade-level or subject-area teachers
- Working with special educators
- Creating differentiated instruction
- Planning teacher-created assessments
- Implementing district and state assessments
- Analyzing and using assessment results to plan instruction and assign student grades
- Attending professional development meetings
- Taking on adjunct responsibilities around the school (for example, as a member of the Safety Committee, Student Study Team, or Shared Leadership Council)

Adaptive P.E. Teacher

Adaptive physical education teachers manage activities, games, sports, and rhythms to meet the needs, interests, abilities, and limitations of students with disabilities. The teacher in this role provides these students with an opportunity to engage in physical activities safely and successfully. The students are able to participate in either the activities of the general physical education program or a modified program in a general education class. The role of the adaptive P.E. teacher includes the following:

- Learning about and understanding students' needs
- Adapting the P.E. curriculum to fit those needs
- Training to teach children with a variety of physical and intellectual abilities
- Providing an environment designed to develop and improve student capabilities
- Adjusting the equipment or game rules to accommodate special needs

Special Education Teacher

The special education teacher holds special credentials and is trained in adapted instructional methodologies for working with students with special needs (physical or emotional) or who have a learning disability. These teachers typically have a self-contained classroom with children who have specific disabilities. Some teachers provide services to students within a mainstream classroom or on a pull-out basis. A school can have several classes for special needs students. The role of the special education teacher includes the following:

- Assessing the needs of students
- Supporting the district instructional program for the student's educational goals or Individualized Education Plan (IEP)
- Documenting observations
- Reviewing and updating the student's educational history
- Conferencing with the student's teachers (if in a pull-out situation)
- Evaluating the student's academic performance
- Reporting findings, participating in classification, and assisting in the planning of IEPs
- Working with classroom teachers of mainstreamed students
- Educating and serving as a resource for the school

Instructional Technology Teacher

An instructional technology teacher, typically someone with a technology background, may be designated to run and maintain a computer lab where students have computer-oriented lessons and activities. The role of the instructional technology teacher includes assisting the classroom teacher and students in the following:

- Learning the basic functions of the computer
- Learning to type and use computer software
- Selecting quality websites
- Navigating the Internet for research
- Supporting current classroom curriculum themes

Administration

Principal

The school principal is the leader of the school. The role of the principal includes the following:

- Identifying the expectations placed on the school
- Ensuring that district guidelines are met
- Managing the faculty and their professional development
- Facilitating parent involvement
- Overseeing the office and support staff
- Managing and allocating the school budget

The principal's role may also include the following:

- Helping develop a shared vision and school mission statement
- Understanding the socioeconomic, cultural, and social issues of the school community
- Nurturing a school culture conducive to learning
- Establishing shared learning goals and helping teachers align their teaching strategies to meet those goals
- Evaluating teachers

Vice-Principal

The vice-principal (or assistant principal) assists the principal in the overall administration of the school. The role of the vice-principal is typically defined by the principal to complement the principal's role in a way that meets the needs of the school. Some vice-principals have designated roles in areas such as discipline management, attendance, the referral process, and special education. The role of the vice-principal may also include the following:

- Scheduling classes, the school day, and special events
- Coordinating the curriculum
- Overseeing professional development
- Ordering supplies
- Overseeing and scheduling the support staff
- Organizing volunteers
- Planning fund-raisers
- Overseeing emergency preparedness and safety
- Evaluating teachers
- Supporting standards of behavior established by the school and classroom teachers

Office Staff

The office staff handles the logistics of operating the school, and typically knows what is going on in all parts of the school. It is important to know the role of each member of the office staff—they are not interchangeable. Following are descriptions of the staff positions found in a typical school office.

Office Secretary

The office secretary assists with paperwork on each student. In larger schools, secretaries may be assigned to specific grade levels or clusters of students. Office secretaries wear many hats and play a large part in making it possible for teachers to do their job. The role of the office secretary may include the following:

- Tracking attendance
- Creating school communications and correspondence
- Managing student records
- Assisting with copying

Office Manager

The office manager oversees the office operations and is the administrator's right-hand person. The office manager also has direct responsibility for significant areas of the school operations. The role of the office manager may include the following:

- Processing payroll
- Distributing school supplies
- Scheduling substitutes
- Supervising the office staff
- Scheduling for the administration
- Scheduling field trips and transportation

Office Assistant

The office assistant generally supports both the secretary and the office manager. The role of the office assistant may include the following:

- Answering the phone
- Distributing communications
- Performing filing and record keeping
- Typing documents
- Making photocopies
- Collecting money for fund-raisers

Instructional Support

Curriculum Coordinator

Some schools have curriculum coordinators to assist teachers with training and implementation of instruction. These coordinators, who learn the curriculum, its implementation, and methodologies, may have responsibilities at both the school level and the classroom level. The role of the curriculum coordinator may include the following:

School Level

- Scheduling and pacing instruction
- Designing and managing implementation
- Planning subject area assessment, and summarizing and sharing assessment data

- Contracting for and conducting professional developments
- Selecting the curriculum
- Aligning the curriculum to state standards
- Collaborating at the district level

Classroom Level

- Assisting with schedules for program implementation
- Using data to form and reform groups
- Considering, and reconsidering, how curriculum resources can best be used in individual classrooms
- Designing plans for instruction of the whole group, as well as plans for needs-based instruction and intervention
- Observing and providing feedback
- Modeling lessons

Bilingual Coordinator

The bilingual coordinator oversees language acquisition of English language learners. Adjunct teachers may fill this role. The role of the bilingual coordinator may include the following:

- Providing individual and group guidance for English learners
- Serving as a liaison for the school
- Advising parents and school personnel on helping students with educational and social challenges
- Planning activities and demonstrating lessons
- Providing classroom guidance activities and schoolwide guidance programs
- Preparing information for students' cumulative records

- Contributing the necessary data for the school's total educational plan
- Facilitating initial placement and/or program enrollment of new students
- Administering mandated testing for English Language Development (E.L.D.) level placement and advancement
- Maintaining the school's compliance at the district, state, and federal levels

Teacher Assistants

Teacher assistants (TAs), sometimes called teacher aides, provide support for classroom teachers. Depending on budget allocations, a teacher assistant may be assigned to more than one teacher. It is important to utilize teacher assistants to their full potential. Too often, teachers assign busy work—such as copying, filing, and prepping lessons—to a teacher assistant. While this is helpful, it is also important to ask the teacher assistant to assist with direct instructional support. Keep in mind that because teacher assistants are not credentialed, only the teacher can provide direct instruction. However, there are many things that a teacher assistant can do to support that instruction.

Additionally, a teacher assistant may be assigned as one-to-one support for students with special needs. In this case, the teacher assistant may be limited in the type of assistance that can be offered, as the purpose is to support the assigned student. The role of a teacher assistant may include the following:

- Assisting students in learning
- Providing students with individualized or small group attention and instructional reinforcement
- Assisting with class business, such as grading tests and papers, entering grades, checking homework, posting work, taking attendance, filing, and making copies
- Reading with students
- Supporting special education students, English language learners, and students who may need remedial modifications
- Observing and/or recording student performance
- Setting up equipment and preparing materials for instruction
- Supervising students in the cafeteria, on the playground, in hallways, and on field trips

Grade-Level Teams

Grade-level teams are a vehicle for coordination and collaboration among teachers by grade level, though the extent of it will vary by school. Your school may formally schedule grade-level release meetings so that teachers can plan together. This sharing of ideas by grade-level teams can be very productive, though some teachers may not want to participate, and it is important to respect their decisions. Be an active participant with the grade-level team, but don't push an agenda on those who don't participate. The role of grade-level teams may include the following:

- Planning for units, parent nights, and field trips
- Articulating record keeping
- Planning and pacing lessons
- Sharing best teaching practices
- Aligning with state standards
- Answering questions
- Opening classrooms for an exchange of ideas
- Demonstrating and observing lessons
- Sharing materials and ideas
- Listening

Student Study Team

A student study team (the name varies according to district and school) typically includes the classroom teacher, nurse, administrator, counselor, and parent of a struggling student who has academic or social concerns. The student study team is assembled as needed, with its composition dependent on the staffing at the school.

The team serves as an intervention resource when all attempts made by the teacher within the classroom setting have failed. The student study team can make recommendations and modifications, as well as referrals for testing. It should reconvene for follow-up and planning of subsequent steps within a predetermined period of time.

Librarian

The school librarian manages the library and teaches basic library skills to the students. The role of the librarian may involve the following:

- Teaching students the difference between types of books, such as fiction, nonfiction, poetry, and biography
- Instructing students in how to use the library system for finding books and other materials
- Encouraging use of the library for information and recreation, while making it an interesting and important part of the school day
- Getting students excited about reading
- Conducting story read-alouds for younger students and arranging special programs for older students
- Teaching research techniques
- Teaching how to access and use the computer database, reference books, indexes to periodicals, and other materials
- Suggesting specific sources or ways of finding information to individual students

Occupational Therapist

The occupational therapist helps referred students better access the classroom and be successful in the standard learning environment. The occupational therapist may assist students with handwriting (fine motor skills) or organizing their materials, thus enabling them to participate fully in classroom learning. Students are usually referred to an occupational therapist as part of an IEP and continue in the program until their specific goals are met.

Speech Pathologist

The speech pathologist assists referred students in speech production, fluency, cognitive communication, and language. A speech pathologist may rotate among several schools. Students are usually referred as part of an IEP and work with the speech pathologist until their specific goals are met.

Counselor

The school counselor assists referred students with personal issues and/or adjustment problems they may be having at school. Students are usually referred by teachers or as part of an IEP. Counselors can be an integral part of the school, although not every school, because of size or budgetary constraints, has a counselor. As students move into high school, counselors may do vocational counseling. The role of a counselor may include the following:

- Behavioral intervention
- Group therapy
- General counseling
- Staff development

Psychologist

The school psychologist collaborates with the teacher and parents to help students succeed academically, socially, and emotionally. A school psychologist may serve several schools in a shared position. The role of the psychologist may include the following:

- Administering formal assessments (psychological and educational tests) and making observations of the student's learning and adjustment in school
- Planning and making recommendations for interventions with referred students
- Generating formal write-ups and/or reports

Nurse

The school nurse may be assigned to one specific school or may serve several schools in a shared position. The nurse can evaluate students for physical problems that may be interfering with learning and can be an integral part of the referral process. The role of the nurse may include the following:

- Monitoring day-to-day issues and complaints of students
- Administering first aid
- Monitoring and administering medication
- Leading staff developments on health issues
- Educating students on health issues

Attendance Counselor

The attendance counselor monitors student attendance and follows up with students and parents on truancy issues. Not all schools have an attendance counselor on staff; the responsibility for this role is sometimes assigned to a designated secretary. It is up to the teacher, however, to handle the initial follow-up on absences whenever possible.

Custodial Staff

The custodial staff is an integral part of the school's success. The custodial staff is usually managed by the plant manager, with staff members assigned to designated buildings and/or responsibilities. Smaller schools may have only one person on the custodial staff, while larger schools often have a custodial staff of several people. The role of the custodial staff includes the following:

- Maintaining the school facility
- Cleaning the school facility
- Stocking the school with supplies, such as paper towels and soap

Take time to get to know the custodial staff member who is assigned to your classroom. Establish a relationship of respect, which helps create a partnership of support. Your class should do its part in cleaning and maintaining its own space. The role of classroom teachers and students in this partnership may include the following:

- Sweeping daily
- Emptying trash and recycling
- Maintaining a clean sink area
- Cleaning desktops
- Maintaining classroom organization and neatness

Parents

Parents can be one of the teacher's greatest assets. Communicating clear expectations to parents on a consistent basis helps build a supportive relationship with them.

Communicating with Parents

There are many ways to communicate with parents. Suggestions include the following:

- Weekly, bimonthly, or monthly newsletter home
- Teacher's website
- E-mail (Use your school e-mail address, not your personal one.)
- Phone calls home (To maintain professionalism and to avoid revealing your personal phone number via caller ID, use the school phone.)
- Inviting parents to visit the classroom
  - Set boundaries, with designated times and days.
  - Parents must always sign in at the office.
  - Check school and/or district policies.
- Requesting parent volunteers
  - Volunteers need school and/or district clearance.
  - Check school and/or district policies.
  - Volunteers usually need medical clearance (for example, negative TB tests).
  - It may be better for parents not to volunteer in their own child's classroom, but in another classroom at the same grade level.
- Weekly progress report (Use the **Weekly Progress Reports** template for this purpose.)

49
Weekly
Progress
Reports

141

Involvement at Home

Homework Support

A significant way for parents to support their
child at home is to be involved with their child's
homework. Homework is a means of
communication between the classroom and the
home. Make an effort to help parents understand
the homework that has been assigned and why
it is important. When parents monitor their
child's homework, they are more informed about what their child is learning.
When deciding on homework assignments, consider the following ideas:

- Homework may serve several purposes.
  - Review and practice
  - Preparation for the following day's class
  - Greater exploration of subjects than classroom time allows
  - Expanded learning by applying skills that students have
    been exposed to
  - Integrated learning by applying different skills, such as
    book reports or science projects
  - Development of good study habits, organization, and
    responsibility
- More homework does not equal better homework.
- Homework should be able to be completed in a reasonable
  amount of time.
- Students need homework that they can complete independently, since
  some parents may not be available or able to assist.
- Homework should be modified to meet the students' needs and skill levels.
- For advanced students, challenge problems can be substituted for assigned
  problems. In this manner, all students complete the same number of problems,
  but advanced students will have more challenging problems.
- Check the school and/or district policy on homework.

The appropriate amount of homework depends on the age
and skills of the students. Kindergarten through second grade
students can benefit from 20 to 30 minutes of homework
each school day. Third through sixth grade students can
benefit from 30 to 60 minutes of homework each school day.

Encourage parents to support their child at home by doing some or all of the
following:

- Offering a quiet place at home or the public library to complete assignments
- Encouraging older and younger siblings to do their homework at the same time

- Using a timer to motivate finishing homework in a timely manner
- Having their children complete homework before engaging in other activities (such as watching television, playing outside, using the computer, or playing video games)
- Encouraging their children to read for 20 to 30 minutes each day

Involvement at School

Parent volunteers at school can be invaluable and can make your job easier in many ways. The key to success is establishing clear boundaries and a specific schedule, together with a well-defined set of responsibilities. Direct instruction and discipline are your responsibility—parent volunteers are part of the support team. The parent volunteer's role should be monitored to ensure that these boundaries and responsibilities are respected. Know the policies with regard to parent volunteers in your school or district. Following are several ideas for including parents in the classroom and/or school:

- Encourage parents to visit the school to meet you, the school counselors, the librarian, the technology instructor, the administration, and the support staff (including teacher assistants, bus drivers, office staff, and school security), all of whom contribute to their child's safety and academic success.
- Open your classroom to parents one morning a month or invite them to have lunch at the school once a month. Topics for discussion can include homework, helping with their child's behavior issues, long-term projects, technology access, physical education, and nutrition.
- Communicate with parents regularly about their child's grades. Invite them to observe the class to see their child in his or her natural learning situation. This gives parents a clearer impression of their child's ability to grasp concepts and work with their peers.
- Make positive calls home, not just negative ones. Teachers often phone home only when reporting inappropriate behavior or academic concerns. Calling with a good report can go a long way toward building a supportive relationship with parents.

- Invite parents to attend school functions. Nearly all schools have Back to School Night, parent-teacher conferences, and other activities that allow parents to learn more about their children's teachers and classroom experience. Students can write reminder letters inviting parents to these functions.
- Invite parents to be involved through the following activities:
  - Joining the PTA
  - Attending school board meetings
  - Chaperoning field trips
  - Helping raise money for the class and/or school
  - Volunteering to assist with student activities

Check the school or district policy on parent involvement for guidance on what parents can and cannot be asked to do. If you can tell parents a specific task you need help with, they may be very willing to help when asked. Don't assume that parents won't help at school just because you know they are busy outside of school. They may still be able to help for one to two hours a month, perhaps before or after school. Help from parent volunteers is especially important when budgets are being cut and teacher assistants and support staff are stretched thin. All you have to do is ask.

Most parents work inside or outside the home, sometimes at more than one job, and they may not be available during school hours. If parents aren't able to be physically present at school, they may still be able to help in other ways. Consider asking parents to help in the following ways:

- Making a small donation (for example, a snack or a package of paper)
  - Send home a Classroom Wish List.
  - When asking for parent volunteers, always include "other possible ways to help our classroom."
- Donating a service (for example, sewing costumes, sorting and stapling readers or packets, or creating name tags)
  - Projects could be sent home and completed as parents have time.
  - Survey parents about their talents and hobbies so you know who might be able to help with special projects.
- Making phone calls for the classroom phone tree

7 Planning, Instruction, and Assessment

One of the key goals of effective classroom management is successful instruction. Planning, instruction, and assessment are therefore essential elements of your classroom management system.

Being prepared is vital to the successful delivery of instruction. Planning your lessons—not just day by day, but for the entire year— helps you accomplish your goals. Planning is an ongoing process, and you will constantly be making adjustments in what and how you teach. Every class has its own unique background and particular needs for the year. Assessing those needs regularly helps with effective planning and allows you to make adjustments and modifications to your plans as needed.

For a new teacher or a teacher at a new grade level, planning the first year of teaching a particular body of material is an investment. As you gain experience teaching, it becomes easier to prepare your lessons year by year. Three templates, **Lesson Plan: Open-Ended**, **Lesson Plan: Direct Instruction**, and **Lesson Plan: Into-Through-and-Beyond**, can be used to help plan your lessons.

In this chapter, we introduce ways to help you plan what and how you teach your students, how you assess them, and how those assessments affect your planning for future instruction.

19
Lesson Plan: Open-Ended
20
Lesson Plan: Direct Instruction
21
Lesson Plan: Into-Through-and-Beyond

Planning

To begin your planning for specific lessons or units, ask yourself a few questions:

- Where do you want your students to go?
- How do you want your students to get there?
- How will you know that they achieved what you want them to?

As you think about the answers to these questions, keep in mind that they form the basis for organizing your lesson plans. Use the following headings and content examples to guide your planning with regard to state content standards, goals, objectives, materials, and lesson plan procedures.

State Content Standards

Determine the grade-level state standards that are to be covered in the lesson or unit you are planning. Be sure to include all the standards that apply, since many lessons in your unit link across the curriculum and therefore include more than the main subject area.

Standards can be reworded and specific skills can be isolated for a more student-friendly approach. For example, if students are asked to create a time-ordered sequence writing piece, the official standard might read as follows:

1.0 Writing Strategies
Students write clear, coherent sentences and paragraphs that develop a central idea. Their writing shows they consider the audience and purpose. Students progress through the stages of the writing process (e.g., prewriting, drafting, revising, editing successive versions).

    1.3 Use traditional structures for conveying information (e.g., chronological order, cause and effect, similarity and difference, posing and answering a question). [English-Language Arts Content Standards for California Public Schools, Kindergarten Through Grade Twelve]

These content standards could be rewritten in more student-friendly terms as follows:

- Students will write a story in chronological order.
- Students will write a story in sequential order.
- Students will write a story in time order, using "first," "next," "then," or "last" at the beginning of each sentence or paragraph.

Goals

Goals help you decide the purpose of a lesson or unit. These usually draw on state or national subject-specific standards. In basic terms, what do you expect students to be able to do by the end of this lesson or unit? If we work from the previous example, we might articulate goals in one of the following ways:

- The purpose of this unit is for students to understand how to use time-ordered sequence for a variety of occurrences in everyday life. This will be achieved by using a timeline, organizing pictures from a familiar story, writing an essay, and more.
- The purpose of this lesson is for students to describe daily occurrences in their lives by writing an essay in time-ordered sequence.

Objectives

Objectives focus on what your students will do in order to attain the knowledge and skills required to meet the state and/or national standards. The objectives for your lesson or unit plans are directly related to the content standards.

For daily lessons and/or the unit, determine what the students will be able to do during the lessons or unit. State specifically how they will accomplish this and what the satisfactory attainment of the objectives will be. For example, objectives might be articulated in either of the following ways:

- By the end of the unit, students will be able to demonstrate their understanding of time-ordered sequence through a series of related activities, such as using a timeline appropriately, placing pictures from a story in order of their appearance in the book, writing a time-ordered essay related to daily life, and more.
- By the end of the lesson, students will be able to write a four-paragraph essay using time-ordered sequence, to describe at least five daily experiences from the time they wake up in the morning until the time they go to bed at night.

Prerequisites

Prerequisites take into account your students' background knowledge. As you prepare a new lesson or unit, think about what students should already be able to do before each lesson is taught. If students don't have the necessary knowledge or skills to meet the lesson's objectives, you will want to provide them with prerequisites for the new lesson— activities that will prepare them for learning the new knowledge or skills. Considering prerequisites allows you to plan scaffolding activities for each lesson to make sure that students can meet the objectives.

Front Loading

There may be times when a small group of students could use some preteaching or introductory exposure to a lesson before it is taught to the class as a whole. For example, English language learners may need to have key vocabulary introduced before the lesson, or students with special learning needs might benefit from small group practice of a skill before you introduce it to the entire class. This front loading helps students who might be at a slight disadvantage to feel more confident when they begin the lesson.

Materials

Being well prepared for teaching a lesson or unit requires that you know exactly which materials you will need in the classroom for each lesson—both for your own reference and for the students. A complete list of books (including textbooks, reference books, picture books, and ancillary resource books), worksheets, workbooks, equipment, art supplies, and other materials is helpful.

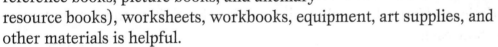

Lesson Plan Procedures

Planning a lesson entails creating a detailed, step-by-step description of how to carry out the lesson and achieve its objectives. These procedures provide suggestions to the teacher for implementation of the lesson plan, including an explanation of what the teacher should ask the students to do during the lesson. The teacher may not follow the procedures in the plan exactly when he or she is actually delivering the lesson, but anticipating details in the planning process makes the lesson go much more smoothly.

Anticipatory Set

In your introduction to the lesson, you need to grab the students' attention and motivate them to be interested in the lesson. This is the "hook"—often a "wow" moment that makes students want to know more. Relate the anticipatory set to something the students already understand. Following is an example of an anticipatory set for a lesson on time-ordered sequencing:

The teacher will share a series of six real photographs of himself or herself preparing for a day at work. The photos will include getting out of bed in the morning, brushing teeth, tying shoes, eating breakfast, making lunch, and getting in the car to leave for school. Each photo will include a description written on a sentence strip. The teacher will have students place the photos in time-ordered sequence, then match the descriptions to the corresponding photos.

Main Lesson Activity

Explain the focus of the lesson and how you will facilitate learning. Include the detailed descriptions of both the teacher's instructional activities and the students' activities. List how each activity will be carried out, step by step. As tedious as it may seem, making this list can be very helpful, and it will ensure that you aren't forgetting anything. You should always perform an activity, such as an experiment, before using it in the actual lesson. Note the specific materials required for each activity. An example of the level of detail suggested for the main lesson activity follows:

1 · After sharing the anticipatory set with the students, read aloud *Enemy Pie* by Derek Munson. Be sure to emphasize several events in the book and have students predict what will happen next as you read aloud. This will establish occurrences throughout the book.

2 · After reading the book, review several of the events from the story as a whole class.

3 · Using five pictures from the story with corresponding descriptions printed on sentence strips, have students help organize the pictures in time-ordered sequence. Remind students to use words like "first," "second," "next," "after," "finally," and "last," where appropriate.

4 · Using a timeline, have students work together in small groups to organize, in time-ordered sequence, five to seven daily occurrences (for example, waking up, brushing teeth, and going to school). Remind students to use the anticipatory set as a reference point.

5 · Once small groups have completed their timelines, have students create individual timelines of their own. These will be used the following day when they begin writing a four-paragraph essay using their graphic organizer.

Modifications

Describe any modifications or adaptations that may need to be made in the lesson in order to accommodate students with special needs, advanced learners, English language learners, and students with alternative learning styles.

Closure

In conclusion, draw the lesson ideas together for students. You may want to ask students what they learned that day (or what they have been learning throughout the unit) to reinforce learning and correct any misunderstandings. Sometimes, these can be charted out and posted, so that students can refer to them when working independently. For example, you might ask, "Boys and girls, what did you learn about sequencing events in time order? What words did you use to do so? Did the pictures help you do this? How?"

Follow-Up Activities

Include homework and/or additional lesson ideas for enrichment. Describe a lesson you might use to follow up this lesson, such as "Students will independently record the events of their evening, from the time they arrive home until they go to bed." or "Students will take home a scrambled story activity sheet and rewrite it in chronological order."

Assessment

You must assess your students' understanding of the objectives of the lesson or unit. This requires you to gather evidence that indicates whether they have completed the lesson or unit in a satisfactory manner or not. An assessment could involve scoring students' work using a grading rubric, a test and answer key, a checklist, or teacher observations, but it must relate specifically to the learning objectives.

More important, you need a clear understanding of how you will evaluate the objectives that were established for the lesson or unit. Make sure you give students the opportunity to practice what you will be assessing them on. Hopefully the assessments will show that your students practiced and mastered what you asked them to.

Final Thought

Your lesson plan should be detailed and complete enough that another teacher who is knowledgeable in the subject matter or at the grade level could deliver the lesson without needing clarification on anything in it. It should be detailed and complete enough that a substitute teacher could come into your classroom and teach the lesson in your absence.

Lesson Plan Book

How do you fit this formal lesson into the limited format of a lesson plan book? While you need to show evidence of planning, you don't need to write formal lesson plans for everything you teach. You do, however, need a record of your lesson that contains enough information to help you successfully deliver it and to satisfy your administrator's requirement of "evidence of planning." Consider including the following basic steps:

- State your direct lesson.
- Include the standards and focus of the lesson.
- List a page or activity for independent work.
- Describe a follow-up activity.
- Develop a system that works for you.
- Be consistent.

Using the time-ordered sequence lesson detailed above, your abbreviated lesson plan book entry could look like the sample lesson plan below. Create an abbreviation system that you will remember and that works for you.

Sample Lesson Plan

Intro: Read: *Enemy Pie*—WG

Strategy: Predict

DL: Review events—WG
   Sequence pics
   (Sequence vocab—"first," "next," etc.)

Act: Sequence timeline—SmG

Ind: Create individual timeline

Day 2: Review; write, using timeline, 4-paragraph essay

KEY

Act	Activity	Pics	Pictures
DL	Direct lesson	SmG	Small group
Ind	Independent work	Vocab	Vocabulary
Intro	Lesson introduction	WG	Whole group

Instruction

One of the toughest concepts for educators—both new and veteran teachers—is how to read the audience and deliver instruction in a meaningful and comprehensive way. The teacher's tone, use of multiple strategies, inclusion of all students, encouragement of student participation, and questioning techniques are all critical components when delivering instruction.

Tone

- **Inflection**—Consider the way you speak to students. Depending on the cultural background of your students, their English proficiency, and their sensitivity, your inflection may play a significant part in how your students respond to you. If you speak in an inviting tone, students will be more likely to participate.

- **Positive approach**—If you speak to students in a positive way and offer reinforcement for a job well done, they will respond positively.

- **Helpful approach**—Know your audience. If a single student is struggling to understand your instruction, consider continuing instruction for the sake of the rest of the class, then revisiting the information with that student while others are working independently. Take a moment to reassure the student that you will revisit the information with him or her later. If you have several students who are struggling, however, it will do no good to continue. In that situation, don't hesitate to stop and clarify, review, reteach, or restate the information, and then move ahead.

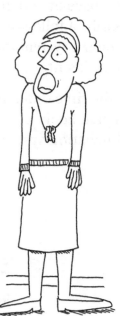

Strategies

- **Hands-on instruction**—When planning lessons, be sure to include a variety of activities that involve hands-on instruction and learning. English language learners (ELLs), students with special needs, tactile learners, and others do well when they can manipulate materials as they acquire understanding.

- **Partner and small group instruction**—Be sure to offer opportunities for students to work in pairs, triads, and small groups. This gives advanced learners the opportunity to take on a teaching role, while struggling learners have models to emulate.

- **Think-Pair-Share**—When you pair students of lower English proficiency with students of higher proficiency, they have the opportunity to share what they have learned with one another in both English and their native language.

Inclusion

- **English language learners**—When you ask for volunteers or call on students randomly, it is important to make sure that English language learners have ample opportunity to participate and share responses in whole class discussions. Front loading vocabulary is a good idea, so that English language learners feel more confident.

- **Special needs**—Students who have an Individualized Education Plan (IEP) or other instructional challenge should not be passed over during question-and-answer sessions. You may want to establish a cue to show when you will question them or give them a heads-up as to what you are about to ask so they will be prepared and confident.

- **Advanced learners**—High-potential and gifted students, who may already know the answer, should not be called on all the time, nor should they be ignored. Be careful not to call on them continually; they can easily dominate a discussion simply because they generally know the answers.

- **Struggling students**—Know your students. If it is apparent that a student doesn't know the answer, don't single him or her out. Be aware of situations when it is important to support a particular student. If you call on a student who doesn't know the answer or gives an incorrect answer, try one of the following approaches:
  - Break the question down into an easier sub-question: "Okay then, what would be the first step in the process?"
  - Shift to another student in a positive manner: "Nice try; who can help [name] out?"
  - Have the entire class answer the question.

Questioning

- **Wait time**—When asking students to respond to questions or ideas, allow sufficient wait time for students to answer. Sometimes they need a few seconds to absorb the question or the information before answering.

- **Higher-level thinking**—It is important to ask questions from easiest to hardest so that students warm up to an idea or concept. Open-ended questions—those that elicit more than a simple "yes" or "no" answer—are a better gauge of a student's understanding.

Bloom's Taxonomy can generate rigor and higher-level thinking within a lesson. These strategies are especially important for gifted and talented education (GATE) students and those who need a challenge. Several strategies often used by teachers to engage students are described at the end of this chapter.

Assessment

There are several ways to assess student learning: summative and formative, check for understanding, pre-tests and post-tests, informal and formal. For a more holistic approach to understanding student achievement, use several different types of assessment in your classroom. An individual student may do well with one type of assessment and not as well with another; this varies by student. Giving your students multiple opportunities to show their understanding evens out the differences between students. Some of the more commonly used forms of assessment follow.

Summative Assessment

At the district and classroom level, summative assessments are an accountability measure that is typically used as part of the grading process. The following are examples of summative assessments:

- State assessments
- District assessments
- End-of-unit assessments
- Chapter tests
- End-of-term exams
- More formal types of assessments

Consider summative assessment as a gauge of student learning at a particular point in time in relation to content standards and an overview of expectations for the material.

Formative Assessment

Formative assessment informs both the teacher and the students about student understanding as the teaching and learning is taking place. This provides an opportunity for the teacher to make modifications in the instruction that can affect the learning process for the students. These in-process modifications help ensure higher student achievement.

Think of formative assessment as practice, often called "guided practice" in lesson planning. Because this kind of assessment is used when new skills and concepts are just being introduced or when students are in the process of learning new material, it does not hold students accountable for that material in grade book fashion. This is just practice—part of an ongoing process. It is often referred to as checking for understanding.

Check for Understanding

Checking for understanding helps you know more about what information students are grasping during a lesson. This gives you immediate feedback so you can adjust the lesson, review, or reteach what is needed before moving ahead. Most of the techniques described below are simple, nongraded, in-class activities that give both teacher and students useful feedback on the teaching-learning process. The following ideas can be used before, during, and after lesson delivery.

Teacher Observation and Questioning

Teacher observation and questioning is the easiest way to check for understanding, and teachers use it throughout the day. It is important to ask questions of all the students. The teacher can use playing cards or Popsicle sticks with students' names; once chosen, a student's name is set aside until all names have been chosen, at which point the teacher starts again. The names of students who have difficulty answering a question can be held for another turn.

Closure

At the end of the period or the school day, or as assigned homework for that evening, ask students to respond to these questions: "What is the most important thing you learned today?" and "What is still not clear to you?" The purpose of this assessment is to obtain information about what students did and did not comprehend in a particular lesson or during the day. Review these responses and use them to guide future planning.

Know, Want, and Learned

A Know, Want, and Learned assessment (KWL) is a great way to check for understanding. Students record what they *know*, what they *want* to learn on a topic, and what they have *learned* about the topic. This not only checks for understanding on what students have learned in the lesson, but it also gives the teacher information about what they knew before the lesson and what their interest level in the topic is.

Pass the Question

On a 5″ × 8″ manila envelope, write a question about yesterday's lesson that pertains to what you are teaching today. Have students pass the envelope around before the lesson begins, while they work on their "Do Now" warm-up activity. Students respond to the question on slips of paper that they place in the envelope. The **Student Response Forms** template can be used for this purpose. Review the responses and use this information to review, move ahead, or plan for future lessons.

45
Student
Response
Forms

Memory Table

Students fill in a table that has columns labeled for topics in a current lesson or unit. For social studies, column labels might be the names of presidents being studied (for example, Washington, Lincoln, and Clinton). Students enter two or three characteristics of each president. Tally the number of correct and incorrect responses, and look for patterns in the incorrect responses in order to plan for areas that need review. To set up the memory table, have students fold a piece of paper to create the number of boxes to be filled in.

Summarizing

Students summarize what they have learned about a topic in a sentence or two, answering the question "Who does what to whom, when, where, how, and why?" The purpose is for students to select only the key concepts of the lesson. Assess the quality of each summary quickly, and note whether students have identified the essential concepts of the topic. Share your observations with your students.

Real-Life Applications

After teaching about a new topic, ask students to write down at least one way to apply this concept in real life. Share some examples and present them to the class.

Student-Designed Test Questions

Allow students to write test questions and model answers for a lesson topic, in a format consistent with ordinary tests. This gives students the opportunity to have a voice in their learning and to reflect on what they understand. It generates a wide range of meaningful questions at all ability levels. The **Student Question Forms** template can be used for this purpose. You may want to evaluate the questions and use the better ones, perhaps with revision, on your actual exam.

44
Student
Question
Forms

Reflection

Planning, delivering instruction, and assessment work in conjunction with one another. Each of these elements needs to be carefully considered before, during, and after a lesson has been taught. Yet reflection on the entire process is as important as any individual part of the planning process, as a means for future application. Use Post-it Notes as reminders for the following year; they can be placed directly into your teacher's edition and can include notes on what worked, what didn't, and what you would try differently.

Aids for Planning, Instruction, and Assessment

Troubleshooting a Lesson

As you plan each section of a lesson, consider the following questions.

Introduction

- What is the purpose of the lesson?
- What are students expected to do or know at the end of the lesson?
- How will you motivate students?
- How does the lesson link to previous lessons?
- How do you plan to deliver instruction?

Instruction

- What materials will be required? Who will pass them out, and when? (This is especially important if you are using manipulatives.)
- How will students be seated? (Will they be seated on the floor, at desks, in a circle, in a U shape, in the gym, out of doors?)
- Do you have a step-by-step sequence of activities in mind?
- What will you need to model in order for students to understand the lesson?

Guided Practice

- How will you keep students engaged throughout the lesson?
- Will students be active participants?
- What clues will you look for to tell you that students are successful?
- What techniques will you use to check for understanding?

Practice

- Will students complete an independent assignment?
- Will students work in pairs throughout the lesson and/or during the practice portion of the lesson?
- What tangible element of your lesson will demonstrate that students have met the learning goals?
- What plans do you have for early finishers?

Modifications

- How will you modify the lesson for English language learners?
- How will you accommodate students with special needs?
- How will you modify the lesson for advanced learners?
- Will you incorporate a multicultural approach?
- Will you need to modify your assessment?
- Will you need to modify your scoring rubric?

Closure

- How will you end the lesson?
- How will you ensure that all students understood the lesson?
- Will you restate the objectives and ask students if they have met the learning goals?

Homework

- Will you assign homework?
- Does the homework support what you taught that day?
- Will you modify homework for English language learners, students with special needs, and advanced learners?

Understanding Your Teacher's Edition

Adopted curriculum series often have many components (for example, softcover books, manuals, CDs, and DVDs) to support instruction. It's easy to be overwhelmed by these, but if you spend some time examining them, they will start to make sense. Not taking the time to review the additional components of the curriculum can limit your effectiveness in conveying the material to your students. The additional components may include the following:

- Homework masters
- Assessment masters
- Strategies and methodologies
- Support for English language learners
- Intervention strategies
- Extension activities

The centerpiece of any curricular program is the teacher's edition (TE). This often has a little bit of everything in it. Generally speaking, most teacher's editions are broken down into the following categories:

- Planning pages
- State standards
- Appendices (overview methodologies)
- Glossary of terms
- Lesson pages
  - Background information and instructional tips for the teacher
  - Objectives and goals
  - Questioning strategies and ideas
  - Explanations of student book pages
  - Extension activities
  - Support for English Language Development (E.L.D.)
  - Challenge support
  - Differentiated instruction ideas

The teacher's edition typically has thumbnails of pages to be used with students. (Depending on the curriculum, these may be included in a separate book instead.) Material in the teacher's edition related to these pages typically includes key terms and explanations of the following:

- Chapter titles, strands, concepts, or unit themes
- National and/or state standards
- Objectives, purpose, and/or goals
- Daily and/or weekly planning

  - Day-by-day breakdown of the strand, concept, or theme
  - State standards related to each lesson, strand, concept, or theme, which are usually embedded in the daily lessons
  - Recommended pacing plan
  - Sample questions and questioning strategies for opening and closing the lesson, as well as for using throughout the lesson
  - Hands-on lesson ideas to model and implement, related to a specific skill or concept
  - Ideas for use of related manipulatives
  - Learning style target activities
  - Subject-specific curricular connections (such as Art, Social Studies, Science, Math, Cultural, Reading, Writing)
- Strategies for meeting the special needs of diverse learners
  - English language learners
  - Special education students
  - Students who are at risk or struggling
  - Advanced learners
- Organized and formal types of assessments (thumbnails)
  - Entry-level assessments (such as diagnosing readiness, warm-up review)
  - Progress monitoring (such as guided practice, mixed review, diagnostic checkpoints, multiple choice cumulative reviews, problem solving)
  - Summative evaluations (such as free-response chapter tests, multiple choice tests, performance assessments, timed tests, CD-ROM practice tests, Internet resource assessments)

- Ideas for assessing content standards (thumbnails)
  - Diagnostic checkpoints
  - Free-response chapter tests
  - Multiple choice tests
  - Performance assessments
- Homework (thumbnails)
- Intervention
  - Reteaching lessons
  - Intervention lessons
  - Intervention practice
- Scope and sequence
  - Breakdown of strands, concepts, or themes by grade level to show where a corresponding element is taught at other grade levels
  - Indication of when an element was last introduced, and the breadth of coverage

Cumulative Records

In order to plan lessons and units effectively, it is essential to know your students—their interests, ability levels, learning styles, cultural backgrounds, whether some have IEPs requiring modifications or accommodations to lessons or units, whether some are advanced learners needing extra challenges, and whether some are English language learners needing language support. It is best to begin with the students' cumulative records (physical or electronic), which contain their academic history. The following information is typically included in the cumulative record of a student:

- Identification data
  - Current family address
  - Current home phone number (cell phone or landline)
  - Schools attended in the past, with dates that the student entered and left
  - Names of teachers for each year (useful if you have questions about the student during the current year)
  - Entry codes
  - Age
  - Grade
  - Days present
  - Days absent (useful in understanding if a child is behind)
  - Yearly picture
  - Health record
  - Home language
  - Social and emotional factors that affect learning

- Report cards and progress reports
  - Academic subjects
  - Work and study habits
  - Learning and social skills
  - Teacher comments
  - Days absent, present, and tardy
- State test records
  - Subject-specific scores
- Bilingual records
  - English Language Development (E.L.D.) level
  - Progress records
  - Work samples
  - Test scores
- Summer school and intervention information
  - Curricular areas in need of support
  - Summer school or intervention location and program
  - Teacher's name
  - Grade level

Individualized Education Plan

If any of your students have an Individualized Education Plan (IEP), it is important to read it so that you are familiar with the student's academic history, the goals that have been met, and any modification or accommodation that the student regularly requires. Because goals are set and reassessed annually, the information contained in the IEP will impact your lesson planning. If you have questions about information found in the student's IEP, you should meet with the school's special education advisor. The following information can be found in a typical IEP:

- Student information sheet
- Present level of performance in the area(s) of need
- Performance and assessment summaries in the area(s) of need
- Annual goals and objectives used for planning and assessment
  - Incremental objectives related to goals
  - Date goals and objectives are projected to be achieved
  - Supports for participation in general education activities
  - Standards-based promotion
  - Variations
  - Accommodations
  - Modifications

- The IEP team recommendation and information summary about goals for the IEP meeting
- Follow-up actions
- Parents' participation and consent

Bloom's Taxonomy

Bloom's Taxonomy, a classification of educational learning objectives, is an excellent tool to help you motivate students and stimulate their thought processes. According to the original Bloom's Taxonomy (Bloom, 1956), human cognitive processes—or levels of thinking—can be grouped into six categories: knowledge, comprehension, application, analysis, synthesis, and evaluation. The updated version renames the categories as follows: remembering, understanding, applying, analyzing, evaluating, and creating (Krathwohl, 2002). According to Lorin Anderson, one of Bloom's students, the names of the major cognitive process categories were changed to indicate action, because thinking implies active engagement.

In practical terms, familiarity with the different cognitive processes described in Bloom's Taxonomy can help a teacher plan lessons that guide the students from one level to another. For example, different types of questions require students to use different cognitive processes, or levels of thinking. A lesson that provides an opportunity for students to be creative and apply what they have learned allows students to become more involved in the learning process, making learning more meaningful and purposeful.

The following overview uses the updated version of Bloom's Taxonomy. A basic definition, word prompts (expressions that encourage that process), and practice (suggested activities that support that process) are listed. Numerous online resources explore each cognitive process in depth.

Remembering

Definition Students respond to show their understanding of what they have learned.
Word Prompts Define, summarize, recall, identify
Practice Paragraph summary, sequencing events, comic strip, report

Understanding

Definition Students share what they already know and have learned.
Word Prompts Tell, list, describe, explain
Practice Timeline, completing a table on a topic, story problems, graphing

Applying

Definition Students put what they have learned into practice.
Word Prompts Demonstrate, solve, make, use
Practice Diorama, model, poster, minibook, role-play

Analyzing

Definition Students interpret what they have learned.
Word Prompts Conclude, interpret, compare, contrast
Practice Graphing, sequence organizing, experiment (trial and error)

Evaluating

Definition Students make a judgment about what they have learned and how they learned it.
Word Prompts Rationalize, defend, uphold, rate
Practice Presenting, scoring with a rubric, defending a project or idea, class discussion or debate

Creating

Definition Students create, using information they have learned.
Word Prompts Design, compose, form, envision
Practice Building a working model, creating a play, designing something related to a topic

What is presented here is a rather simplistic breakdown of Bloom's Taxonomy. You may want to spend more time reading about and understanding the finer points of each cognitive process, so that you are better able to incorporate them into your own classroom.

Gardner's Multiple Intelligences

As you plan engaging and higher-level lessons for your students, keep in mind that every child has a preferred style of learning and obtains new information in a variety of ways. Consider incorporating Howard Gardner's Multiple Intelligences theory. First published in Gardner's book *Frames of Mind: The Theory of Multiple Intelligences* (1983), this model helps teachers understand and teach to different learning styles, personalities, and behaviors. The theory has been embraced by educators and has served as a classic learning model for teachers for many years.

Although most teachers have knowledge of Gardner's model, we present a brief summary of each of the intelligences in a succinct manner. You may want to do some additional research of your own. The following section provides a basic understanding of each of the intelligences. This will help you determine each student's type of intelligence or learning style, best practices to consider, and approaches for planning lessons, delivering instruction, and assessing student understanding of the material.

Gardner's Seven Original Intelligences

Linguistic

Learns best through words and language (journalists, English teachers, translators)

Logical-Mathematical

Is good with numbers, logic, and critical thinking (accountants, scientists, researchers)

Musical

Understands music, sound, and rhythm easily (singers, musicians, entertainers)

Spatial

Learns best from visual images and can visualize well (designers, photographers, engineers)

Bodily-Kinesthetic

Needs opportunities to move and "show" what has been learned (performers, athletes, chefs)

Interpersonal

Considers other people's feelings (counselors, clergy, coaches)

Intrapersonal

Is self-aware and confident (involved in the process of changing personal thoughts, beliefs, and behavior in relation to his or her situation)

Gardner's Three Additional Intelligences

In his later work, Gardner identified three additional intelligences beyond the original seven, though he added only the naturalistic intelligence to his model. Some theorists debate any potential additions to the model.

Naturalistic

Relates to nature and the natural environment

Existential

Comprehends abstract information, without a need for concrete and/or sensory experiences

Moral

Has an affinity to learning about ethics, humanity, and life

Visual, Auditory, and Kinesthetic Learning Styles

Related to Gardner's Multiple Intelligences is a model that focuses on visual, auditory, and kinesthetic learning styles. This model offers simple methods to understand and explain students' preferred ways of learning. It is a helpful guide that should be considered along with several other elements as you plan your lessons, instructional delivery, and assessment.

Visual

Students learn best when they can see and read about what is being taught.

Auditory

Students learn best when they can listen and talk about what is being taught.

Kinesthetic

Students learn best when they can use their senses—specifically touch—to experience what is being taught, and by doing, making, or building.

Most students have a preferred learning style, although they usually learn through a blend of all three styles. A student's learning style is a reflection of his or her mix of intelligences. This will be examined in more depth in Chapter 9, Instructional Challenges.

Final Thoughts

Even as you analyze your students' learning styles and multiple intelligences, remember that you know your students best. Keep their faces and personalities in mind as you plan lessons, instruction, and assessment. Think about their ability levels, their special needs, and how they best retain information. Get to know your students: Find out where they come from, what their interests are, and what they like to do in their free time. All of this will help ensure successful learning in your class. You can relate learning experiences to who they are and what they like as you give examples during instruction.

More important, vary your teaching. Avoid delivering instruction only as lectures and giving the students only paper-and-pencil activities. This approach reaches students with only one learning style. Create lessons that offer multiple opportunities for the various learning styles. This ensures that you will meet the different learning needs that a diverse class presents.

References

Bloom, B.S. *Taxonomy of Educational Objectives: The Classification of Educational Goals. Handbook 1: Cognitive Domain.* White Plains, N.Y.: Longman, 1956.

Dalton, J., and D. Smith. "Extending Children's Special Abilities—Strategies for primary classrooms" (1986). Accessed from http://www.teachers.ash.org.au/researchskills /dalton.htm#Comprehension.

Gardner, H. *Frames of Mind: The Theory of Multiple Intelligences.* New York: Basic Books, 1983.

Krathwohl, D.R. "A Revision of Bloom's Taxonomy: An Overview." *Theory into Practice,* 41(4), 212–18 (Autumn 2002).

Overbaugh, R.C., and L. Schultz. "Bloom's Taxonomy." Accessed from http://www.odu .edu/educ/roverbau/Bloom/blooms_taxonomy.htm.

8 Managing Active Learning

When students are engaged in active learning in a classroom, there is often a muted buzz of activity. It may be that they are working in pairs or small groups, rather than independently and all seated at their desks. Active learning encourages full engagement and participation by all of the students in the class.

It's a challenge to manage active learning and keep students participating and engaged. Some students enjoy working alone, some in pairs, and some in small groups. Most students enjoy a combination of these, often depending on the subject matter. These are important considerations that need to be part of your planning. Managing active learning is an essential part of classroom management, and it can be done effectively with some proactive thinking on your part. In this chapter, we introduce ways to design small groups, activities for pairs and small groups, and suggestions for learning centers to help you with that aspect of your planning.

Teachers must consider how they can best organize students to keep them attentive and motivated. When grouping students, consider the following:

- Ability levels
- Behavior
- Learning styles
- English language development (E.L.D.) levels
- Cultural styles
- Special needs
- Practicality with a specific lesson

Group Work

Group work can be a good way to get students to respond to your direct instruction. While the students are working in their groups, you have an opportunity to circulate, ask questions, and make observations of student progress. This is not a time for you to work on other things.

Designing Small Groups

Successful collaborative student group work depends on the "workability" of your assigned groups. Deciding which grouping arrangement works best for your particular class involves strategic planning on your part. Some options work better for younger students, some for older students. Consider the following:

- Which students work best together?
- Which students can serve as academic and language support for one another?
- Which students will bring out the best in others?

Following are several different approaches for organizing students into small groups. Choose one that enables your students to work well together to complete the group's assignments and tasks.

ABC Order

- Organize students by first or last name.
- Group students whose names begin with A through D together, those whose names begin with E through H together, and so on, depending on how many groups there will be.
- Group students whose names begin with A or Z, B or Y, C or X, and so on.

Captains

- Designate a captain for each team.
- Have each captain select an even number of girls and boys for a team.
- Assign a number to each team.
- Place a slip of paper with each team number in a bowl.
- Have each captain draw a number from the bowl to select their team. (Captains may or may not get the team they put together.)

When you choose students as captains, always be equitable in your approach.

- Be sure you have an even number of girls and boys.
- Don't choose only the most capable students.
- Consider a student with special needs, an English language learner, a student who needs to take on a leadership role, or a student who occasionally misbehaves.

Colored Index Cards

- Using a different color of index card for each group (yellow, pink, blue, and so on), count out as many index cards in each color as you will have students in each group.
- Hand out one index card to every student. All students with a yellow card will be in one group, all those with a pink card will be in another group, and so on.

Count Off

- Determine how many groups you will have for an activity.
- Have students count off until that number is reached, then have them repeat counting off. For example, if there will be five groups, they should count off 1, 2, 3, 4, 5, then start again at 1. Students should write down their designated number or hold up that number of fingers to help them remember their group number.
- Have all "1" students form a group, all "2" students form another group, and so on.

Deck of Cards

- Determine how many students will be in each group.
- Deal a custom deck of playing cards to the students, having included an appropriate selection of number cards, face cards, or cards in a suit to correspond to the number of students in each group.
- Group the students based on shared number cards, face cards, or suits. For example, put all students with a 4 in one group and all students with a 7 in another group; or put all students with a face card in one group and all students with a number card in another group; or put all students with diamonds in one group and all students with spades in another group, and so on.

Pair Line-Up

- Have students form two lines of equal length.
- Have the lines face one another.
- Designate facing students as partners.

Activities for Small Groups

Jigsaw

Activity

- Students work in heterogeneous groups of three to five students.
- Each group discusses a topic or question for 5 to 15 minutes. Suggested topics for discussion include the following:
  - A current story
  - A lecture or lesson
  - A text reading
  - A topic to research on the Internet
  - A newspaper article
- Students have the following responsibilities in the group:
  - One student leads the discussion.
  - One student takes notes.
  - The other students contribute ideas.
- The group then shares its thoughts or findings with the rest of the class.

Use

This is a great activity to use as part of a lesson from a textbook. For example, each group discusses a section of a chapter, answers one of five required questions, or discusses one page of a five-page article. In this way, each group becomes an expert in its assigned area and shares its thoughts or findings with the rest of the class. During the share-outs, all students take notes. The **Jigsaw Organizer** template can be used for this activity.

18
Jigsaw
Organizer

Group Investigation

Activity

- The teacher introduces a unit or theme.
- Students gather in groups to discuss the following:
  - What they already know about the topic
  - What they want to learn about the topic
- All students share their thoughts to be recorded on a whole-class Know, Want, and Learned (KWL) chart or a similar chart.
- Each group chooses one of the "What we want to know" concepts on the chart to research.
- Each group researches its chosen concept and prepares a brief report based on its research.
- Each group designs a presentation to share its findings with the whole class.
- The class discusses each presentation.

Use

This activity uses a student-directed approach, and it is a great activity to use at the beginning of a unit. It gives students some control over what they are learning and gives their learning more purpose. A group investigation activity gives the teacher an opportunity to find out what motivates students about the topic, and thus helps steer planning. The **Group Investigation** template can be used for this activity.

14
Group
Investigation

Four Corners

Activity

- The teacher divides the class into four groups.
- In each corner of the room, the teacher posts a question or idea on large chart paper about a curricular unit.

- Each group rotates through the four corners. The group discusses each question or idea for five minutes, records its responses, and then moves on to the next corner. In each rotation, the group reads the previous group's responses and adds to them.
- After four rotations, the whole class discusses the questions or ideas.

Use

This is an appropriate activity to use for introducing a new unit, to check for student understanding of a current unit, or to assess learning for a just completed unit. It gives students a change of pace and gets them out of their desks and moving around. During the rotations, the teacher can move around the room, asking questions and making informal evaluations of student progress.

Roundtable Discussion

Activity

- The teacher divides the class into small groups.
- The groups brainstorm ideas related to a recent topic.
- After discussion for a specified amount of time, students record their ideas on paper, a transparency, or chart paper to share with the whole class.
- Ideas can be saved and referred to in future group and class discussions.

Use

This activity fosters discussion and can help drive instruction. It can be used to check on student progress and to check for understanding.

Panel Discussion

Activity

- The teacher selects four or five students to act as a panel of experts on a given topic.
- The rest of the students form small groups and develop meaningful questions related to the topic to ask the panel.
- While the small groups are developing questions, the panel can discuss possible questions and formulate possible responses.
- The teacher circulates between the panel and the small groups to facilitate the process.
- The question period depends on the flow of questions to, and responses by, the panel.

Use

This is a fun activity to use after a read-aloud of a book or story, where the panel can act as characters from the story and answer as if they were those characters. This is also a great activity to use as a review of science and social studies units.

Debate Teams

Activity

- Students are divided into two groups, or teams.
- Each team takes one side of an issue or topic.
- Students research and prepare for their team's side of the debate, working independently over a two- to four-day period.
- After two to four days, the teams reconvene. Each team selects two or three debaters for its side, and then develops questions for the audience to ask the other team. The **Debate Organizer** template can be used for this purpose.
- The teacher acts as mediator during the debate, ensuring that the discussion does not get hostile or one-sided. The teacher sets guidelines for conduct and responses:
  - Don't name-call.
  - Use appropriate language.
  - Don't interrupt.
  - Speak only when it is your turn.
- Students in the audience ask questions of the debate teams, which form arguments and respond to one another.

11
Debate
Organizer

Use

This activity can be easily incorporated into social studies and current events units. It combines independent research with collaborative small group work.

Activity for Pairs or Partners

Think-Pair-Share

Activity

- Students pair with a partner to share their responses to a question.
- Students share their responses with the whole class. (You may want to have three to five pairs of students share out.)

Use

This activity is especially useful for English language learners and students with special needs. Be sure that these students are paired with students who are more fluent in English or who are more proficient academically. This activity can be used very informally throughout the day for any lesson: "Okay, I want you to turn to your neighbor and take turns sharing a response for one minute."

Learning Centers

Classroom learning centers help students develop self-monitoring skills and offer them opportunities for exploration. Centers should be a part of the normal classroom routine, be organized in designated areas in the classroom, and include activities for students to engage in at designated times or when their work is completed. Use the **Center Sign-In Sheet** and **Center Tracker** templates to track student participation at classroom centers. Well-organized centers can serve not only as enrichment of the regular curriculum, but also as areas where students can learn new things and be creative on their own.

06
Center
Sign-In Sheet
07
Center
Tracker

- Start with one center, and add others as students become more adept.
- Introduce each center before the students use it, and explain how to complete activities at each center.
- Establish center rules with students, just as you do for the classroom. Rules can be posted at each center.
- Establish a rotation schedule and time limit for students to move from one center to the next. Practice rotating through the centers.

- Make sure that centers support your curriculum and/or offer the opportunity for free exploration.
- You may want to allow students who finish their work early to visit their favorite center or work on an unfinished activity at a center.

Setting Up Learning Centers

Following are learning center ideas that you can easily incorporate into your routine, using the current theme, unit, chapter, or lesson in your curriculum book to guide the activities. These will be illustrated in more depth in Chapter 10, Curriculum Overview.

File Folders

File folders can be used to create centers. The folders can be stored in a file box, from which students can select the folder (center) they want.

- On the outside front of the folder, attach the directions and rules for using the center.
- Inside the folder, place the actual activity (for example, a game board, pictures of guided practice, or a sample of a product). Staple a plastic zipper bag to the folder, and place center pieces or components in the bag.
- On the outside back of the folder, attach a sign-in sheet so that you can track student use of the center.

Plastic Bins with Lids

Plastic bins, which can be found at many discount stores, can be used to store all supplies and materials needed for a specific center. This allows several different learning centers to be used at one designated worktable. Plastic bins are especially helpful for science centers, which often require a large number of materials.

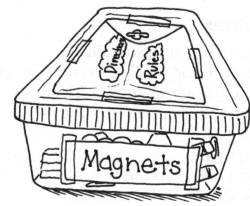

- Label the bins and store them on a shelf near the center worktable.
- On the top surface of the lid, attach a large envelope containing the directions and rules for using the center.

Student Desk with Inside Storage

A student desk can be set up as a center, for example, a publishing center.

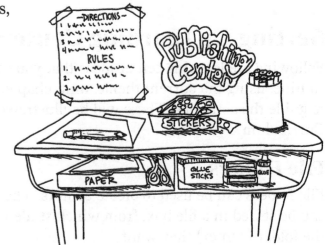

- Inside the desk, store paper and a box with supplies (for example, markers, pencils, glue sticks, and scissors).
- Store containers of art supplies, such as stickers, on top of or inside the desk.
- On top of the desk or on a wall near the desk, post the directions and rules for using the center.
  - Rules should be very explicit, so that students don't use all the supplies at once. For example, you may limit students to one sticker per visit.
- If there are several activities to choose from (for example, story starters), write the name of each activity on an index card and store the cards in an index card box.
- Restock the center frequently in order to maintain student interest.

Curriculum-Related Learning Centers

04
Bulletin Board
Labels

Make sure that your learning centers are clearly labeled. The **Bulletin Board Labels** template can be used for this purpose. It's important that students know which center they are in and what is expected of them at that particular center. Some centers may require specific rules for use. For example, the math center may have rules for using manipulatives and storing materials in their designated boxes; the science center may have rules for conducting experiments; and the computer center may have rules for turning computers on and off and for Internet use.

Math Center

- Counting, sorting, and patterning
- Measurement (weight, height, width, and volume)
- Creating and/or solving story problems
- Creating and/or practicing facts with flash cards
- Tangram patterns
- Timed math facts worksheets
- Using calculators to solve problems
- The problem of the day

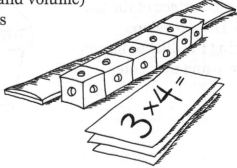

Science Center

- Growing lima beans or other small plants and recording growth over time
- Using magnets
- Disassembling and examining small machines
- Organizing animals according to life cycle
- Sink or float experiments

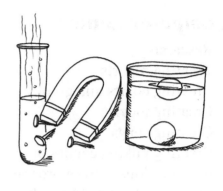

Publishing Center

- Creating a minibook for a current story, unit, or theme
- Designing a comic strip for a current story, unit, or theme
- Completing a story starter
- Writing a poem or rap about a current curriculum concept
- Writing a letter (to a friend, a character from a current story, or a historical figure)
- Creating an invitation to a character from a current story

Rug Center

- Board games (for example, chess, checkers, pattern blocks, and Unifix cubes)
- Building blocks
- Puzzles (big pieces, little pieces, few pieces, and many pieces)
- Electronic learning games (for example, Leapfrog and Hooked on Phonics)

Listening Center

- Books on CD
- Podcasts or stories on MP3 players or iPods
- Recording student readings to play back
- Recording teacher- or student-generated stories (using a computer program such as GarageBand or Mixcraft) to play back

Computer Center

- Research
- Creating reports
- Creating charts and graphs
- Creating movies
- Creating songs
- Creating talking comics or presentations using a program such as GarageBand or Mixcraft
- Editing and printing photographs
- Visiting museums online
- Conferencing with other classrooms or schools
- Creating a webpage
- Creating presentations

Learning Center Rules of Behavior

A good set of rules will provide clear expectations for student behavior in the learning centers, and thus will help your centers run smoothly. Develop the rules for your classroom learning centers together with your students. Some suggested rules follow:

- Treat equipment and materials with respect and care.
- Store documents in folders that the teacher has approved.
- Work only in your designated center.
- Work on the designated activity.
- Don't eat or drink at or near the centers.
- Respect the time limit, so that others can rotate through the center.
- Take turns and work together cooperatively.
- Ask for assistance.
- Report any problems with equipment or materials to the teacher immediately.
- Clean up the space when you are finished, and return materials and supplies to their original location.
- Leave any equipment ready for the next student before you rotate to the next center.
- Advise the teacher of supplies that need restocking.

Consequences

You may want to establish two to five consequences for breaking a rule of behavior at a learning center. For example, the consequences for breaking a computer center rule might include the following:

- You will lose center privileges for a specified length of time.
- You will sit out a rotation.
- You will clean up the center area during recess or lunch.
- A note will be sent home if the infraction is serious.

Make sure that consequences are age-appropriate and written in student-friendly language.

Individual Work

Students frequently work independently on assignments, activities, and projects. The most common form of individual work is called "independent practice," where students complete an assignment relevant to what you taught in class. This can also take the form of working on assignments, activities, and projects when they finish work early.

Activities for Individual Work

Many teachers find it helpful to classify additional individual work in terms of "Must Do" and "May Do."

A "Must Do" activity supports direct instruction and is a follow-up to a lesson. It has a specific purpose and outcome and must be completed before being able to engage in a "May Do" activity.

A "May Do" activity is often viewed as a privilege for finishing all current classwork. It may include exploration that doesn't have a specific goal or intended outcome. The **Must Do/May Do** template can be used for this purpose.

24
Must Do/
May Do

"Must Do" Activities

"Must Do" activities need to be completed after students finish their independent practice. It is important to make "Must Do" activities attainable and either self-sufficient or able to be completed by students assisting one another. There should only be two or three "Must Do" assignments; otherwise, students may not have the opportunity to work on "May Do" activities.

Some suggested "Must Do" activities follow:

- Finish a current essay or writing assignment.
- Practice math flash cards for a specified time (for example, 5 to 10 minutes).
- Complete a social studies map outline.
- Finish reading a Literary Circle chapter.
- Complete a science journal entry.
- Practice designated handwriting sheets.
- Complete a science, social studies, or art project.
- Finish a spelling or grammar assignment.
- Complete an assigned task (for example, writing a friendly letter).
- Work on a social studies PowerPoint presentation.
- Complete a cultural art piece.
- Complete a math practice set.

"May Do" Activities

"May Do" activities often involve centers and free-choice activities that are available to students. Select activities that won't distract other students who are still completing "Must Do" activities.

Some suggested "May Do" activities follow:

- Read silently, or visit the classroom library.
- Use the computer center.
- Use the center of your choice.
- Play a game on the rug.
- Create a clay model.
- Cut out coupons and add up how much you would save for five favorite items.
- Draw a favorite scene from this week's chapter book read-aloud.
- Go to the listening center and listen to the story again.
- Help a friend.
- Help the teacher.

Additional "Must Do" or "May Do" activities, depending on your classroom needs, could include:

- Research projects
- Reader's theater
- Sight word practice
- Timed reading practice
- Fluency practice
- Illustrating vocabulary from science, social studies, or a weekly story
- Partner reading
- A student's own idea

"Must Do" and "May Do" Rules

It is a good idea to establish three to five rules for students who are working on "Must Do" and "May Do" activities. Here are some suggestions:

- Use a quiet voice.
- Avoid interrupting the teacher or other students who are completing classwork.
- Clean up the area before starting a new activity.
- When working with a partner, use a corner in the classroom where others won't be disturbed.
- Stay in the teacher's sight at all times.

Final Thoughts

Thoughtful planning about how your students work individually, in small groups, in pairs, and in mixed groups is essential to managing students' active learning. Keep in mind that students need models, need to be challenged, and need to be partnered with students who will bring out the best in them.

9 Instructional Challenges

Today's classrooms are more diverse than ever. Not only do students come from many different cultural backgrounds, but they also learn in different ways, have a variety of interests, have different levels of linguistic and academic ability, and may have other special needs. This diversity offers a multitude of instructional challenges to the classroom teacher.

> In my classroom, I teach tolerance. I teach that some people don't learn as fast as others, but that perseverance will outshine innate ability. I teach that life is not fair, but that you can work with the cards that you're dealt with to find success. I teach that what you say and how you act is more important than the way you look or the way you talk. I teach that we can all contribute something positive to the lives of those we interact with. I teach that we all learn best by correcting our mistakes. I try to teach my students how to respect themselves and each other. After that, I try to teach some chemistry.
>
> *David Tomerlin, Los Angeles*

In order to be able to meet these challenges, you must get to know your students, learn about your students' needs, and tap into their strengths. In this chapter, we provide an overview of many of the instructional challenges that you will encounter in your classroom. With a better understanding of the diversity of your students, you will be able to incorporate modifications into your classroom management that will facilitate learning. You may want to begin by finding out about your students' preferred learning styles.

Different Learning Styles

Students take in learning in a variety of ways. Some learn best through auditory means, while others do best when they can experience instruction in visual terms. Still others more easily meet their potential when they have opportunities for hands-on activity. Teachers must consider ways to address all students and approach planning and instruction in ways that engage and motivate every student in the class.

Best instructional practice offers multiple opportunities for learning that incorporate the three main learning styles so that all students can be engaged. Although this isn't possible with every lesson, it is important to strive for. Keep in mind that some students are strong in more than one learning style, while others may have a strong preference for one style over the others. Providing students with experiences and opportunities to interact on multiple levels and to present what they have learned allows them to be successful.

Visual Learners

Visual learners learn by seeing the information that is being taught. They benefit from instructional input that includes the following:

- Reading
- Flashcards
- Posters, charts, and visual aids
- Videos
- Demonstrations
- Making lists and diagrams

Auditory Learners

Auditory learners learn by listening to the information that is being taught. They benefit from instructional input that includes the following:

- Discussions
- Oral presentations and lectures
- Audio CDs
- Music
- Videos
- Expressing verbally what they are learning

Kinesthetic Learners

Kinesthetic learners learn by combining physical activity with the information that is being taught. They benefit from instructional input that includes the following:

- Hands-on projects
- Physical activity and movement
- Role-playing and acting
- Practical applications

Modifications

The basic modifications that follow work for nearly all students. For those who struggle academically due to language difficulties, special needs, or weaknesses in certain academic areas, additional strategies specific to the needs of that particular group of students are included, which may help you teach in a style that will meet your students' needs.

Getting Students Started

- Let students know when you are starting a lesson and how long it will take from beginning to end.
  - This gives specific start and end points to struggling learners and those with a negative attitude toward the subject being taught. Stick to the plan: If you share the time frame with students, you need to keep your word.
- Break the lesson down into segments if the subject area is daunting.
  - For example, you may specify 5 minutes for the opening, 10 minutes for direct instruction, 10 minutes for group work, 15 minutes for independent practice, and 5 minutes to share out as a whole class.
  - You may want to use a timer to track the lesson, possibly designating a student to monitor the time.

Keeping Students Engaged

- Include students in the lesson.
  - Make the lesson participatory, hands-on, inclusive of Specially Designed Academic Instruction in English (SDAIE) strategies, routine, step-by-step, full of modeling opportunities, multicultural whenever possible. Most important, include students' interests and learning styles. These simple ideas make lessons relevant to students.
- Keep distractions to a minimum.
  - This is especially important if you have several struggling students who are easily distracted.
  - Keep bulletin boards simple and orderly, and avoid hanging student work from the ceiling.
- Keep students' desks free of clutter.
- Redirect off-task behavior.
  - It's helpful to give some students a squishy ball to hold during lectures or a coffee straw to chew on, so that their attention is directed toward you (in combination with the ball or straw) rather than on other students or the view out the window.

- Give positive feedback to students who are engaged and participating appropriately.
  - This is especially important for students who are progressing toward Individualized Education Plan (IEP) goals, language development, and/or behavior modifications.

Keeping Students in Their Seats

- Make sure that every student understands the rules about individual desk seating, floor seating, and gathering in groups. Students with special needs or language difficulties may need constant reminders about this.
- For students who feel the need to walk around, who find their desks and chairs confining, or who are kinesthetic learners and need to be mobile, consider the following ideas:
  - Stretch breaks
  - An individual desk, with the desk and chair sized appropriately for that student
  - Option of standing during lectures
  - A behavior plan that rewards students for remaining in their seats for a given amount of time
- Have students use signals to request permission to leave their seats.
  - American Sign Language (ASL) signs can make a request specific but not distracting, for example, "R" to signal that the student needs to use the restroom, "P" to signal the need to sharpen a pencil, and "D" to signal the need for a drink of water.

Keep distractions to a minimum, and have students be very specific about their out-of-seat requests.

Helping Students Follow Directions

- Be direct and clear about what is expected of all students. To avoid confusion, post step-by-step directions and use as few words as possible. This is especially important for English language learners and students with special needs.
- Call on students to repeat directions back to you. You might call on more advanced students to do this as a model, but also call on struggling students to repeat directions for everyone to hear.
- Role-play directions, depending on the subject, the activity, group needs, students' ages, or class dynamics.

Additional Modifications

All of these ideas will improve your everyday, basic approach to planning, instruction, and student participation. However, there are many other, more specific ideas for modifications that can be incorporated as well. Several suggestions for additional modifications follow:

- Allow students to work in homogeneous pairs or groups.
- Allow students to complete work at home if they cannot finish it in class.
- Allow students working independently to wear silent headphones to block noise.
- Allow students to use a computer to write their assignments if they have difficulty using pencil and paper.
- Check for understanding with individual whiteboards.
- Use a timer to track assignment periods. If necessary, extend the time allowed for assignments.
- Have students track their reading with a highlighter or index card.
- Include classroom breaks in addition to recess and lunch during the day.
- Incorporate visual aids, realia, and SDAIE strategies in your lectures.
- Vary the formats of tests.
- Modify rubrics for scoring students' work.
- Offer models or samples of completed assignments.
- Provide a special study area, a special study time, or special partner arrangements.

- Reduce the number of math problems, essay paragraphs, steps in a poster presentation, or number of words on a spelling list for children with special needs.
- Transcribe student stories as they are related to you.

Working with Students with Special Needs

It is essential for the teacher to set the tone for an inclusive environment, where every child has equal access to the curriculum and participatory practices, and all students' needs are considered and addressed in planning, instruction, and assessment. In setting the tone for an inclusive environment, if you hold high expectations for all students, they will hold them for one another and for themselves. If you treat everyone fairly and equally, they will follow your lead.

An inclusive environment is important for all students, especially those who present instructional challenges, whether the challenges are cultural or linguistic or relate to special needs, learning styles, or ability levels. It is important for students who may often be marginalized, who are rarely regarded as part of the whole group, or who don't feel that they fit in. An inclusive environment is also important for those who fit the traditional student mold, in that they are given the opportunity to explore and appreciate the different ways their classmates learn, as well as to work with students with whom they share similarities.

There may be misconceptions or a significant lack of understanding on the part of the general education teacher regarding students with special needs. In such cases, the teacher may struggle to create the inclusive environment that students are entitled to. Many students demonstrate behavior typically labeled as special needs. Making sense of these labels is much easier if a child has an IEP with specific benchmark goals in place. However, this is still difficult if the general education teacher has little background or experience with special needs. It can be even more confusing when the student has not been formally diagnosed, but exhibits behavior that coincides with that of students who have IEPs.

In a typical inclusive classroom, students with special needs are included in the general education setting with students who do not have special educational needs. Inclusion can require many modifications to the general curriculum, and most schools use it only for selected students with mild to moderate special needs. Other schools rely on the mainstreaming approach, where students are part of both the  general education classroom and the special education classroom, depending on their needs. In the mainstreaming approach, students are typically in the general education classroom for specific time periods based on their skills, and a special education teacher provides their instruction the rest of the time.

Whatever your school's approach or your personal philosophy, knowledge, or experience in meeting the needs of students who require modifications, the following ideas can help you get started and can serve as useful tools for all students, not just those with special needs. These ideas can be easily incorporated into any lesson plan, classroom organization, or delivery of instruction.

- Use mixed ability grouping, in which you organize students in learning and working groups where they can support one another, for example, those who are weak in specific subject areas can observe those who are more adept.
- Give students a copy of your lecture notes. This avoids students having to copy from the board or chart paper, which can be distracting, or having a situation where students get off task as they struggle to transfer information.
- Use a variety of graphic organizers to help students classify data.
- Maintain clutter-free bulletin boards. A simple presentation avoids distractions for students with special needs.
- Use Post-it Notes to remind students how much time they have to complete an assignment or to remind them of appointments, for example, with the special education teacher or school counselor.

- Provide a way for students to track required assignments and homework for the day or week. This can be in the form of a checklist or bullet points.

- Use visual aids and provide concrete models whenever possible.
- Keep instructions to a minimum. Provide a list of directions or steps, either on the board or on a sheet of paper. This prevents overloading the student with too much information at once.
- Color-code required materials. For example, attach a strip of green tape to the science textbook and mark any additional science materials (for example, manipulative boxes or students' subject-specific journals) in green.

- Allow extra time to complete assignments if necessary.
- Incorporate a listening center for reading and language support.
- Clarify instructions, repeat steps, and make sure students know what is expected of them.
- Use preferential seating, such as desk placement or permission to sit at the teacher's table, when students need extra help.
- Circulate to a student's desk when extra help is needed.
- Seat students away from distractions whenever possible.
- Provide references on students' desks (for example, multiplication charts, science terms for the current unit, spelling or vocabulary lists, and cursive writing samples).

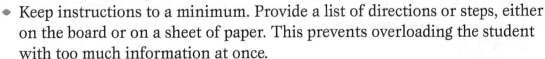

- Have an isolated desk available for students who feel the need to work alone on specific tasks.
- Allow students to give oral responses instead of written ones, illustrations instead of words, and timelines instead of paragraphs (when appropriate) to demonstrate understanding of a concept.

Most teachers are not qualified to make a medical or professional diagnosis of special needs. They can, however, be alert to possible indicators of learning-disabled students, even if the students have no IEP in place. Following are some indicators:

- Struggling with short-term and long-term memory
- Being easily confused or frustrated
- Low self-esteem
- Being easily distracted
- Inability to stay on task for long periods of time
- Struggling with self-control
- Inability to get along with others in and out of the classroom
- Difficulty in remembering directions
- Stubbornness
- Difficulty in handwriting

What follows is a description of the more common special needs identified in today's classrooms, and a simple guide to use in considering whether or not a student might benefit from being tested. If past education strategies have not been working for a student who has already been tested and has an IEP in place, the strategies detailed below may help you know how to move forward with that student as well.

Students with Learning Disabilities

Understanding Students with Learning Disabilities

A learning disability indicates that a child's ability to receive and process information is different in some way from that of the typical student. Although these students are often just as bright as their peers, they experience difficulty learning in school under traditional teaching methodologies. Some students might have more than one specific learning disability. Students with learning disabilities may struggle in one or more specific subject areas, most commonly in reading, writing, spelling, or math. They may also struggle with recalling, remembering, and organizing.

Strategies for Working with Students with Learning Disabilities

- Seat the student close to the front of the classroom, near the teacher (preferential seating).
- Break directions down into smaller steps.
- Repeat directions.
- Provide outlines.
- Provide extended time for reading, assignments, and testing.
- Break lessons into smaller assignments.
- Provide small group or one-on-one work.
- Provide alternative, hands-on projects.

Students with ADD or ADHD

Understanding Students with ADD or ADHD

Attention deficit disorder (ADD) is typically defined as inattention and impulsivity for one's age group. A child with ADD has difficulty focusing for any length of time and struggles to control himself or herself. Attention deficit/ hyperactive disorder (ADHD) is defined as inattention and impulsivity combined with hyperactivity. A child with ADHD is in constant motion, in addition to having difficulty focusing and struggling to control himself or herself.

Children diagnosed with ADD and ADHD struggle in processing neural stimuli. Almost everything in the child's environment is perceived as stimuli: Everything the five senses experience bombards the brain so that the child has no time to process or respond before the next stimulus occurs.

Children with ADD or ADHD have much to offer, and these traits should be tapped into and not overlooked. These children are often creative, flexible, and enthusiastic about learning, and they have great energy. Using these traits to advantage will help the teacher make school and learning more enjoyable. The instructional challenge of ADD or ADHD is not indicative of students' intelligence or talent, since many of them are intellectually or artistically gifted.

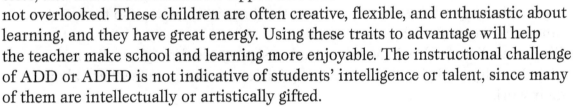

Characteristics of Students with ADD or ADHD

Students with ADD or ADHD may struggle with the following:

- Sitting still
- Staying in their seats
- Staying focused on tasks for any length of time
- Writing—getting their words written down and formatted properly and neatly
- Self-control
- Speaking out in class, or speaking out in class only at appropriate times
- Staying in line
- Saying the right things
- Speaking up for themselves
- Taking time with and/or completing their work

Strategies for Working with Students with ADD or ADHD

If you have students in your class who are diagnosed with ADD or ADHD, or students who show signs of these disorders, consider the following ideas to make your classroom responsive to their needs.

- Learn as much as you can about the students. Check their cumulative records to see if there is an IEP with benchmark goals, listing strategies that have worked in the past. If so, you can benefit from that.
- Offer a few choices during the day for completing assignments or tasks. When students have choices, and when assignments or tasks are more manageable, students have more of an investment in doing their work well.
- Use technology when appropriate. Let students use word processing software to complete their writing assignments, and let them spell-check on the computer. This keeps their fingers busy.
- Break down directions into small steps and have students repeat them back to you. You may even want to write out the directions or steps so that students can check them off as they are completed.
- Give immediate feedback. Monitor students' progress throughout the lesson, period, or day, and give them direct, explicit, and immediate feedback about their work.
- Incorporate a variety of independent practices and assessments into your planning. It is acceptable for students to show their understanding of concepts in alternative ways, as long as you can assess their understanding.
- Ask for assistance from the special education coordinator, the students' parents, or your administrator. Keep in mind that it is the students' success you are concerned with, not the fear of asking for help.

Students with Autism

Understanding Students with Autism

Autism is a developmental disorder that affects the brain's normal development of social and communication skills. It begins to be noticeable in the first three years of life.

Characteristics of Students with Autism

Students with autism may struggle with the following:

- Pretend play
- Social interactions
- Verbal and nonverbal communication
- Sensitivity to the five senses
- A change in routine
- Keeping their bodies still
- Letting go of specific objects (literally and figuratively)

Strategies for Working with Students with Autism

- Be consistent; avoid changing expectations and causing confusion.
- Role-play situations so that students not only hear what is expected of them, but can also see it.
- Incorporate rules using details to explain. Modeling these rules several times is helpful.
- Plan student work to coincide with the number of minutes you know they can be attentive.
- Allow students to use the computer to type their words; to dictate to an aide, who can transcribe students' thoughts; or to use magnetic letters to spell out words.
- Teach social skills explicitly. Model social skills several times while bringing attention to the character trait being addressed.
- Know what sets a student off, and avoid pushing the particular buttons that set a student off whenever possible.
- Make sure that the students have scheduled breaks, which might be more frequent than for other students.
- Offer opportunities for turn-taking and waiting. If possible, use a visual cue to signal these opportunities.
- Offer choices whenever possible.
- Share successes with the students and their families.

Students with Asperger's Syndrome
Understanding Students with Asperger's Syndrome

The main symptom of children with Asperger's syndrome is difficulty with social situations. Symptoms can be mild to severe: The spectrum of symptoms is vast, and no two children with Asperger's syndrome are alike. Keep in mind that a child with one or two of the symptoms listed below does not necessarily have Asperger's syndrome.

Characteristics of Students with Asperger's Syndrome

Students with Asperger's syndrome may struggle with the following:

- Understanding social signals, such as reading body language and taking turns during a discussion
- A change in routine
- Showing empathy or compassion for others
- Understanding speech tone, pitch, and accent
- Eye contact
- Recognizing and interpreting facial expressions and gestures
- Social boundaries, such as talking too much about a favorite topic and not letting others speak
- Neatness, especially in handwriting

Strategies for Working with Students with Asperger's Syndrome

The individual needs of children with Asperger's syndrome vary, but the following strategies can be helpful:

- Provide a clear structure and set a daily routine. Keep the same agenda every day.
- Point out the distinction between a finished product and one that will be completed over time.
- Provide several warning cues about a change in routine or a transition to a new activity.
- Use clear language. Avoid the use of clichés, which can be confusing.
- Address the student individually and directly.
- Repeat directions and check for understanding.
- Deliver instruction in a variety of ways and tap into different learning styles.
- Teach social rules directly.
- Minimize elements that could be distracting, such as loud colors on walls and students' work hanging from the ceiling.

Students with Emotional and Behavioral Disorders

Understanding Students with Emotional and Behavioral Disorders

Emotional and behavioral disorders are more prevalent in today's classrooms than at any time in the past. These disorders are evident when a student displays a continual pattern of behavior that results in disruption of the teacher and other students. While this behavior pattern has likely been manifested throughout the student's life, there is no single way to measure social or emotional functioning. Unless you are professionally qualified, withhold judgment until proper testing can be done. Check the student's cumulative record; if the student has an IEP, look for comments from past teachers with regard to the pattern of behavior you have observed.

Characteristics of Students with Emotional and Behavioral Disorders

Students with emotional and behavioral disorders may struggle with the following:

- Withholding aggressive reactions toward others when provoked
- Avoiding bullying, threatening, or intimidating behavior when frustrated
- Avoiding being physically abusive toward others
- Avoiding destruction of others' property
- Showing empathy and concern for the feelings of others
- Showing remorse
- Taking responsibility, blaming others for their own misdeeds instead

Strategies for Working with Students with Emotional and Behavioral Disorders

- Always inform students what is expected of them, even if this becomes repetitive.
- Avoid threats.
- Show a sense of fairness, and enforce classroom rules consistently.
- Build students' self-confidence whenever possible.
- Maintain a sense of structure with the curriculum and classroom agenda.
- Expose students to others who exhibit appropriate behaviors.
- Offer direct instruction when correcting misbehavior to help students master appropriate behavior.

- Determine consequences for misbehavior and apply them from the beginning. Include students in the process of establishing rules and consequences, so that they are invested in it and understand what will happen if they break the rules. Be sure to administer consequences immediately.
- Use time-out strategies to redirect disruptive behavior.
- Acknowledge the contributions of students when appropriate.
- Provide encouragement on a consistent basis.
- Praise good behavior or performance immediately after it occurs, as a way of reinforcing it.
- Be patient, sensitive, fair, and consistent, and a good listener.

Students Who Are Gifted

Understanding Students Who Are Gifted

Students who show high potential in one or more subject areas can be an interesting challenge to teachers. These students finish assignments quickly and correctly, ask for more challenging work, and/or get bored easily. They need activities and projects that offer creativity and higher-level thinking.

Characteristics of Students Who Are Gifted

Students who are gifted may exhibit the following:

- Great curiosity
- Active imagination
- Ability to give responses that go above and beyond
- Ability to remember and retain much information
- Ability to understand complex concepts
- Excellent organizational skills
- Excitement about sharing facts and research
- Ability to learn independently

Strategies for Working with Gifted Students

- Have students design questions and research topics of their own choosing.
- Offer open-ended activities to be researched and studied, then shared.
- Encourage students to consider many possible answers and to approach questions with a critical eye.
- Ask students to take on leadership roles that require social interaction.
- Offer students opportunities for independent reading of age-appropriate books that require deeper thinking.
- Have students read about subjects they are interested in.
- Provide long-term projects that allow students to study and research over time.

Unfortunately, it is easy to neglect students who have high potential. These students usually complete work on time, consistently participate, and offer higher-level thinking responses. Because they do well and finish work early, they may find themselves bored, and they sometimes go without the attention they need. Gifted students must be challenged and tended to, just like any other student in the class. The following ideas can help you plan challenging activities beyond regular classroom assignments:

- Students can develop minibooks, based on current science, social studies, math, or story concepts.
- Students can design a poster that demonstrates a current science concept, math strand, or social studies timeline.
- Students can construct a crossword puzzle using current spelling words or vocabulary in a subject area.
- Students can write and illustrate a poem based on a closed format.
- Students can design a movie poster that introduces characters, the plot, and a setting in a way that entices others to want to see it. The imaginary movie can be based on current learning.
- Students can critique three designated subject-related websites.
- Students can design the front page of a newspaper, with headlines and stories about what is happening on the school campus.
- Students can construct a clay model of a famous piece of art, a science-related concept, or a historical figure or place.

Working with English Language Learners

It is becoming more common to have students in the classroom who are English language learners (ELLs). They need support, not only in understanding the curriculum in English, but also in learning English. The goal is to transition these students into a full English classification, while advancing them academically. This can be quite a challenge and is often overlooked.

An inclusive environment in the classroom is essential to making sure that all students feel safe and welcomed and willing to take risks, and it is perhaps especially true for students who are learning English and need the support of their teacher, peers, and parents.

The following sections describe the different levels, or stages, of English Language Development (E.L.D.), together with a list of strategies that can help English language learners in the mainstream classroom. Keep in mind that different districts and states may have their own classification system for the process of transitioning students from their native language to English.

E.L.D. Levels

Level 1

- Has very limited to no English language ability
- Points and nods to respond
- Illustrates to communicate

Level 2

- Has limited English language ability
- Gives yes/no responses
- Is in the early stages of writing and uses inventive spelling

Level 3

- Has some English language ability
- Gives short-phrase responses
- Writes simple sentences

Level 4

- Uses the English language with few errors
- Can discuss topics
- Writes complete sentences with few errors

Level 5

- Is fluent in the English language
- Can discuss topics fluently
- Writes like a native speaker of English

E.L.D. Strategies

- Specially Designed Academic Instruction in English (SDAIE)—Layer lessons to review vocabulary and concepts in order to meet students' specific needs.
- Sheltered English—Make academic English comprehensible to English language learners.
- Total Physical Response (TPR)—Incorporate physical responses from students into lessons as much as possible.
- Realia, visual aids—Use tangible items and posters.
- Preteach/reteach—Preteach lesson vocabulary to enhance comprehension of the lesson, and reteach lessons for reinforcement.

In addition to the strategies just mentioned, the following suggestions will help you work with English language learners in your classroom. They can be used throughout the day and across the curriculum.

- Present lessons clearly, speak more slowly, be animated, and use hand gestures.
- Model lessons and activities.
- Guide students through lessons and activities.
- Use games that build language and interaction.
- Use choral reading.
- Practice dictation.
- Introduce books on CD.
- Role-play.
- Use graphic organizers, summarizers, and outlines.
- Place students of different E.L.D. levels in cooperative groups for support.
- Provide hands-on learning opportunities.
- Post vocabulary, for example, on a word wall.
- Provide sufficient wait time for students to formulate answers. Be patient.

E.L.D. Series

It is important to use an adopted curriculum that has been specifically and purposefully designed to support English language learners. This may often be forgotten or ignored, since it takes extra time and some creative planning to incorporate it into an already full day. However, it is critical to English language development and should not be overlooked. The following strategies may help:

- Designate a period every day for English as a Second Language (E.S.L.) instruction.
- Partner with another teacher to group students of similar E.L.D. levels.
- Align lessons to your curriculum, if possible.
- Designate a specific time in the school day when it works well for the whole class for you to work with the E.L.D. series with your English language learners—after lunch, during independent practice time (after a lesson), or at the end of the day.
- Introduce the E.L.D. series to the whole class, then divide the students into smaller groups. While you work with English language learners, native English speakers can do more extensive activities based on the lesson.

Diversity of Students

Students with special needs, English language learners, students who are gifted, and those with different learning abilities and styles are often heavily considered when teachers are involved in planning lessons, delivering instruction, and making assessments. When meeting the needs of these groups of students, teachers simultaneously meet the needs of all students.

Today's diverse classrooms also encompass a variety of cultural backgrounds. In considering a culturally conscious curriculum and creating a space where all students are welcomed, teachers may want to consider the following.

Communication with Families

If you think you might need a translator when speaking with the parents of a student, request one early enough so that he or she is available at a face-to-face conference or a phone call home.

Relating to Students

Become familiar with your students' comfort level in interpersonal communications. Know whether a student is comfortable being called on and whether he or she is comfortable with physical contact, such as high-fives, side hugs, or a pat on the shoulder. Some students aren't comfortable with direct eye contact when talking to another student or when being reprimanded. Some students may find it uncomfortable to shake hands, use gestures, or point.

Disposition

Some students respond best to formal interactions; they may show signs of subservient behavior that could suggest disinterest but that are, in fact, an indication of respect. Be sure you understand the difference before you make a judgment about a particular student.

A Welcoming Space

Create a space that is inviting, caring, and respectful, one where students feel comfortable sharing with the teacher and the class. Don't call on any student as if he or she were representing a cultural element being discussed in class. For example, don't ask a student who has emigrated from Cambodia if he or she agrees with a statement in the textbook about Cambodia. This may put the student on the spot and make the learning environment uncomfortable for that student and for the whole class.

Diversity and the Curriculum

The teacher must consider not only students' special needs, learning styles, and language needs when planning instruction, but also the cultural diversity of the class. This includes, but is not limited to, students' race, culture, and religion. It is extremely important to have an equitable curriculum where all students' backgrounds are considered and respected. Keep the following considerations in mind when planning curriculum, instruction, and discussion.

- The curriculum should not be watered down.
- Culture is not only about race.

- All students should be considered, not just students of color.
- Devoting one month of the year to a particular cultural group is not enough to meet the diverse needs of all students in the class.
- A sense of equitability should be maintained.
- Students should be given ample time to dialogue and share.
- The teacher should be open to various perspectives.

Final Thoughts

In addressing the instructional challenges presented by the diversity of the students in your classroom, it is essential to set the tone for an inclusive environment. As you work with each individual student, be sure to keep detailed notes, seek advice from your team members and administrators, work closely with special education teachers, conference with the student, and stay in touch with parents. You may want to use the **Anecdotal Log** template to record and track students' progress. Each student's needs can best be met when everyone involved works together, with as much transparency as possible.

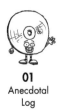

01
Anecdotal
Log

10 Curriculum Overview

Managing a classroom means managing students' learning of the curriculum. In your classroom, students will study age-appropriate curricular areas that build on prior knowledge and lay the foundation for new material. Thus it is imperative that you understand how to effectively manage the content for each curricular area for the students assigned to your classroom.

In this chapter, you will learn about the different age groups and what students need to learn at each grade level. The major curricular areas are analyzed, and strategies and resources that can be an integral part of instructional delivery are presented. A variety of teaching ideas and useful websites are introduced. When you know your curriculum and you are able to effectively plan strategies that are appropriate for the grade level and age of your students, the classroom can run more smoothly and there should be fewer discipline issues.

As a start to getting to know your students and what they'll be learning at the various grade levels, consider the following questions:

- Who are you teaching?
- What needs to be taught?
- How are curricular areas subdivided?
- What tools are useful for each curricular area?
- What strategies can be used to manage different learning styles and/or levels?

Understanding Who Your Students Are

Who are you teaching? And what needs to be taught?
Before actual instruction takes place, it is important to consider the audience. This section gives a brief overview of students at each grade level and the learning that takes place at that grade level. Keep in mind that students vary in personality and maturity at every grade level, and that states' content standards vary. Consider this overview as a "sneak peak" at what you might expect. Be sure to address your own state's content standards when planning lessons.

Kindergarten (5–6 Years Old)
Who

Kindergarten students are typically curious and active. They tend to have short attention spans and are just beginning to develop fine motor skills. They need step-by-step guidance, and they need to have procedures modeled for them many times. They enjoy singing, dancing, and pretending. Their world tends to revolve around themselves. During this period in their lives, they are learning the basics, such as how to share and how to get along. This is an important year to lay the groundwork for appropriate social behavior.

What

Reading

Generally, kindergarten students are learning letters, sounds, and the basics of reading. They are learning that print has meaning. They are acquiring knowledge, from consonant-vowel-consonant (CVC) words to developing simple sentences. They enjoy having stories read to them, and they enjoy reading repetitive simple text, parts of a story, and rhyming patterns.

Writing

Kindergarten students are starting to form words and build from initial dictation to writing simple sentences. They learn to write their first and last names. Their spelling can be inventive, building into simple spelling patterns. They use pictures, letters (both upper- and lowercase), and a limited number of words to communicate.

Math

Kindergartners are counting to 30 and writing, adding, and subtracting numbers from 1 to 10. They do a lot of patterning, comparing, ordering, and sorting by quantity and attributes. Spatial relationships and physical differences (top, bottom, behind, larger, smaller, etc.) are also new knowledge. They identify shapes (square, rectangle, triangle, and circle) and distinguish planes from solids. Time concepts (today, a week, a month) and telling time to the hour are introduced. They use a calendar and learn about coins (penny, nickel, dime, and quarter). Kindergarten students learn to graph objects and pictographs and understand tallying.

Social Studies

Today vs. long ago is a typical kindergarten concept. Kindergartners learn about their national history, patriotism, national symbols (the flag, the eagle), and citizenship. They learn about their community, community helpers, and who they are. This age group learns about cooperation, responsibility, and friendship. In addition, they study simple maps and globes and learn about holidays and famous Americans. They also acquire the concept that money buys goods.

Science

Kindergartners consider making observations of
the world around them as well as knowing physical
properties and attributes. They experience that water
can be a solid, liquid, or gas. They study the concepts
of sink vs. float, plants vs. animals, the life cycle,
weather, shadows, and seasons. They learn about land forms and water forms.
They discuss natural resources (for example, wood vs. man-made).

First Grade (6-7 Years Old)
Who

First graders are still learning how to multitask. They can focus
on a task at hand and work in groups. They seek validation
for their work and can be sensitive to what others think.
They enjoy learning through different experiences, such as
hands-on activities, games, stories, and singing. First graders
are still developing their basic social skills and need
opportunities to practice sharing and getting along. There
is a big transition between kindergarten and first grade, where
they have their own desks, take on more responsibility, and do
more homework. First grade lays the foundation for developing
study skills and learning behaviors.

What

Reading

First graders work toward reading 60 words per minute
and develop increased fluency and comprehension.
They continue learning letters and sounds with
increasingly more complex spelling patterns (short
and long vowel spellings), word families, and rhyming.
Sight words, compound words, contractions, synonyms,
and antonyms are a large part of their skill study.
Reading involves simple sentences, repetitive text patterns, stories, and picture
books. Word attack skills and decoding play an important role in their mastery
of reading. They enjoy having stories read to them, and are able to identify parts
of a story or a book.

Writing

First graders move from simple sentences to paragraphs (stories of several sentences; narrative, expository, and friendly letters). They develop their manuscript handwriting (printing), as well as punctuation and capitalization skills. They learn the writing process for drafting and editing work. They use simple parts of speech (noun, verb, adjective, and adverb) and possessive nouns and pronouns. First graders add details and description to their writing.

Math

First graders count to 100. They add and subtract to 20, and eventually to 100 with no regrouping. Place value (ones, tens, hundreds) is an important part of their math learning, as are ordinal numbers to ten (tenth). They continue patterning, sorting, and comparing ($>$, $<$, $=$), as well as counting by twos, fives, and tens. They do simple graphing, identify shapes and solids, and measure simple lengths, volume, and weight. First graders learn about money (penny, nickel, dime, quarter, half-dollar, dollar), then learn to add and compare values up to one dollar. They work with the calendar. They carry out simple fractional parts (half, fourth). They master addition and subtraction facts up to 10. They compare shapes (number of sides or corners) and tell time (hour, half hour). First graders work with bar and picture graphs, and they use tally charts.

$$3 + 2 = 5$$

Social Studies

First graders learn about their place in time and space. They continue to study family, the community, and community helpers. They learn about their role as citizens, following rules, democracy, and contributing to a group. They learn about fair play and rules. First graders look at the past vs. the present. Maps (and their symbols) are important, as are the concepts of location, weather, environmental influences, daily life, clothing, and diet. In addition to American patriotic symbols and practices, famous Americans and legends are studied at this grade level. First graders learn that diverse communities (ethnic, religious, etc.) are united by common principles. They learn that money can purchase goods and services.

Science

First graders learn from observations of the world
around them and data collection, using simple
sentences and drawing. They study states of matter,
simple machines, weather, the effects of the sun,
the life cycle, and the characteristics, parts, and needs
of plants and animals. They learn about the sun and earth (rotation, orbit)
and the importance of reducing, reusing, and recycling to conserve resources.

Second Grade (7-8 Years Old)
Who

Second graders solidify primary skills in both learning and
socialization. They review and expand on the first grade
curriculum. Second graders are growing up. They are becoming
more independent and self-confident, but they still seek validation.
They are conscious of others around them and work well in
groups. They are becoming more aware of their surroundings
and environment, including material things. Because they are more
self-assured, they also take more risks. Second graders are curious
in their understanding of how and why things work. They are
emerging into young students and defining more of who they
are. When they leave second grade, they have a good grasp
of fundamental skills in math, reading, and writing.

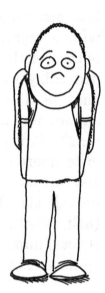

What

Reading

Second graders are working toward reading 80 words
per minute. They read with increased fluency and
comprehension, and they understand complex text for
meaning, purpose, and enjoyment. They have an easier
time with compare and contrast. They learn how to read
and write poetry. They learn to analyze, compare, and
predict text. Second graders identify parts of a story (setting, plot, characters).
They engage in complex spelling patterns (diphthongs, special vowels), word
attack skills, decoding, and sight words. They learn about abbreviations, plurals,
synonyms, antonyms, and cause and effect.

Writing

Second graders develop more detailed stories, with a beginning, middle, and end, using the writing process. They learn to write narratives (personal experience) and friendly letters (parts of a letter). Their sentences are complete, with correct punctuation (commas, quotation marks), subject-verb agreement, spelling, and grammar.

Math

Second graders understand numbers from 1 to 1000. Adding and subtracting to 100 with regrouping is typical at this grade level, as is place value to 1000 and counting to 100 by twos, fives, and tens. Ordinal numbers to 20 (twentieth), comparing numbers ($>$, $<$, $=$), and fractions (half, third, quarter, eighth, tenth) are skills they learn more thoroughly. They also learn about equivalent fractions; planes vs. solids; finding simple perimeters; adding, subtracting, and counting money; and solving transactions up to three-digit numbers. They understand more complex concepts related to money, such as coins and bills (penny, nickel, dime, quarter, half-dollar, dollar), adding, and comparing values up to $2.00. They learn simple multiplication, data graphs, tally charts, range, and mode. Second graders learn measurement (inches, centimeters), time to the quarter hour, and temperature to the nearest ten degrees (Fahrenheit, Celsius).

Social Studies

Second graders study timelines, family trees, maps (title, legend, compass rose, scale), urban vs. rural, community and government laws, patriotic symbols, and economics (producer, consumer). They expand learning about their own citizenship and voting. They study contributions from the past that influence the present (China, Egypt, Native Americans). They study important historical figures. Second graders continue to learn about maps of the world, the globe (seven continents, four oceans), the map of North America, and local and state maps and geography. They also learn more about natural vs. capital resources. Multiculturalism is a major learning experience at this grade level.

Science

Second graders explore and observe change, stages of life, and life cycles. They explore gravity, motion (push, pull), magnets, sound (vibrations), rocks (physical properties, weathering), soil, and fossils. They explore solids, liquids, and gases, as well as resources like rocks, plants and soil, fruits and flowers, and their roles in our lives. They learn about basic weather patterns.

Third Grade (8-9 Years Old)
Who

Third graders are ready for the next level of skills. They tend to be enthusiastic about their learning. They are socially aware of others, their moods, and their differences. They desire acceptance from others. They are more aware of popularity, music, and current trends. Third graders are more apt to test limits and boundaries, and take more risks. They know more about who they are, and what they like and dislike. They are mature enough to take responsibility for their actions and are more reflective. Third grade is the bridge between upper and lower grades at the elementary school level.

What

Reading

Third graders are working toward reading 110 words per minute. They are using phonics, word parts (prefixes, suffixes), and context clues to read and derive meaning. Reading for understanding and information in fiction, nonfiction, biographies, and autobiographies; answering questions; predicting; and interpreting text are some

higher-level reading experiences that they engage in. More chapter books and stories from around the world are introduced in third grade. Reading independently for longer periods of time is also encouraged. Using resources such as a dictionary, thesaurus, encyclopedia, and the Internet makes reading more comprehensible for third graders.

Writing

Third graders learn cursive handwriting. They use the writing process to write paragraphs with topic sentences. They focus on details, correct spelling, punctuation, subject-verb agreement, verb tense, person, and capitalization. They easily use a dictionary and thesaurus. They write narratives, descriptions, and friendly and formal letters, using several paragraphs.

Math

Third graders count and understand place value to 10,000. They learn rounding to the nearest ten, hundred, and thousand; adding and subtracting with regrouping to 10,000; and multiplication and division facts to 12. Third graders learn to determine unit cost and use higher-level thinking and problem-solving skills. They learn about basic probability of outcomes, add and subtract fractions with like denominators, understand equivalent fractions and decimals (tenths, hundredths), and solve problems using money (dollars and cents) up to $5.00. They also study the metric and U.S. customary units of measure for length, volume, and weight. They identify attributes of polygons, quadrilaterals, triangles, and solid forms. Third graders learn to find area and perimeter and to tell time within the nearest five-minute interval. They also learn more about temperature (Fahrenheit, Celsius).

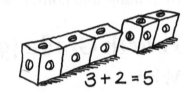

Social Studies

Third graders study immigration in America and abroad, cultural diversity, and the role of different cultures in the United States. They learn about the early exploration of America, local government, laws and rules, and economics (resources to produce). They revisit national and local symbols, study the map as a research resource, and look at geological features of local regions. Native American nations and their interactions with settlers are also studied, along with the impact on the region for settlers in terms of religion, economics, traditions, and contributions. Third graders learn about production of goods and services, basic government laws and principles, and famous American heroes and their role in United States history, especially with regard to freedom.

Science

Third graders engage in scientific investigation and incorporate the tools needed to do so. They review forms of energy (stored, heat, motion) and matter (solid, liquid, gas; atoms to elements). They study the properties of light and how it travels. Rocks and
minerals are reviewed. Simple machines and their uses are examined. They study environments and ecosystems, adaptations of animals and their relationships to one another (herbivore, predator, etc.), and how animals survive in their environments. They learn about patterns and cycles of nature, including the water cycle. They study soil (types, role in plant growth). Third graders study the sun, moon, planets, stars, and their positions in the sky. Human and natural events as they influence species and survival are studied, as well as energy resources (renewable and nonrenewable).

Fourth Grade (9–10 Years Old)
Who

Fourth graders continue to mature. They understand humor better. They are more aware of ability levels and the similarities and differences between themselves and other students. They compare their work to that of fellow students. Fourth graders have a better sense of self-worth and their place in the world than they did a year earlier. They are more introspective and can carry on deeper conversations about the consequences of actions. Fourth graders are independent and enjoy opportunities to solve problems and to investigate why and how things work.

What

Reading

Fourth graders are working toward reading 130 words per minute. They read fiction and nonfiction text both for a purpose and for pleasure. They engage in research by using the Internet and additional resources for informational text. They understand elements of text (figures, tables, pictures, etc.) and apply them to meaning.
They derive the meaning of new words from previous word knowledge, prefixes and suffixes, root words, and context clues. They use a dictionary and thesaurus. They use prior knowledge and text elements to connect ideas and comprehend

new information. They are able to compare and contrast different forms of writing, and they collect information in order to distinguish fact vs. opinion.

Writing

Fourth graders use the writing process to develop multiparagraph essays and compositions, including supporting sentences about the topic or central idea with facts, details, and descriptions. They use correct spelling, grammar, punctuation, and capitalization. They include quotations and citations to support their writing. They use and understand the elements of resources such as the dictionary, thesaurus, encyclopedia, and Internet for writing. Fourth graders write narratives, responses to literature, expository essays (informational reports), poems (rhymed, unrhymed), and summaries with a clear focus and purpose. They write in cursive.

Math

Fourth graders understand and compare ($>$, $<$, $=$) whole numbers to the millions. They add, subtract, multiply, and divide whole numbers and decimals to two places. They order fractions (like and unlike denominators), decimals, and mixed numbers. They round to the nearest ten, hundred, thousand, ten thousand, and hundred thousand. They compare equivalent fractions and decimals, and add and subtract fractions with like and unlike denominators. Fourth graders explore concepts like factoring prime numbers; using a number line with positive and negative integers, fractions, mixed numbers, and decimals; using variables in an expression or formula; and explaining range, median, and mode for data. They continue to solve basic probability problems, find area and perimeter, and describe geometric solids, quadrilaterals, and triangles by attributes. They compare lines (perpendicular, parallel, intersecting), study metric units of measurement, and learn conversions between metric and U.S. customary units of measure.

Social Studies

Fourth graders learn about the history of their home state. They study the United States Constitution, state and federal government, and the roles of elected officials. They continue learning about geography and maps (latitude, longitude), state and regional history, prominent locations, regional divisions, and their state flag.

Science

Fourth graders learn about electricity (simple circuits) and magnetism (repel and attract, earth's poles, compass). They study energy as heat, light, and motion. They discover more about habitats, the food chain, and food webs, as well as about the producers, consumers, and decomposers of an ecosystem. They learn how plants and animals adapt to ecosystems. They work toward an understanding of the basic anatomy of a plant, including reproduction and photosynthesis. They learn more about rocks and minerals, including their formation, types, and properties. They study erosion, change in land formations, and other factors that affect these changes (wind, ice, water, earthquakes, etc.).

Fifth Grade (10–11 Years Old)
Who

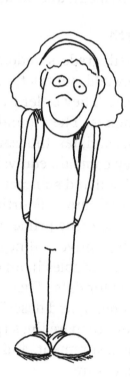

In many school districts, elementary school ends at fifth grade. These students are on the verge of leaving the elementary school, yet they are still very much children. They can handle more independent work and can work for longer periods of time. They understand sarcasm, but are sensitive as to how they are perceived in the world. Conflict can arise over friendships and loyalties. Fifth graders understand the differences between boys and girls much better than they did the year before, and they can even be gender biased. In addition, they are beginning to be more interested in members of the opposite sex. Fifth graders thrive on projects that allow them to be original in their ideas and thinking. They are more responsible and can be given more opportunities for leadership roles. They can be challenged more with problem-solving.

What

Reading

Fifth graders are typically working toward reading 140 words per minute. They read fiction and nonfiction text. They can more easily interpret poetry. They use prior knowledge, comprehension strategies, and inference to understand text. Their understanding of words, prefixes and suffixes, and context clues to derive

meaning is more advanced. They use additional aspects of text to understand what they are reading, including diagrams, tables, and charts found in a selected text. They more quickly understand the main idea, key concepts, symbolism, literary devices, cause and effect, compare and contrast, and intention of the author of a selected reading.

Writing

Fifth graders use the writing process to write narratives, research reports, persuasive letters and compositions, and responses to literature that are several paragraphs in length and have a clear focus and intention. They use purposeful writing to describe, inform, entertain, and explain. Their use of grammar, spelling, sentence structure, punctuation, details, and voice in writing is stronger. Their word attack skills, understanding, and use of context to derive meaning are better. They write in cursive and use a keyboard more fluently. Fifth graders use resources such as a dictionary, thesaurus, encyclopedia, and the Internet to research, gather, and clarify information.

Math

Fifth graders are quickly adding, subtracting, multiplying, and dividing whole numbers (multidigit, long division), decimals through the thousandths, fractions (like and unlike denominators), mixed numbers, and positive and negative integers. They round from millions down to thousandths. They plot fractions, decimals, mixed numbers, and positive and negative integers on a number line. Graphing, plotting with four quadrants, and ordered pairs of integers (x and y) on a grid are used as they select and plot appropriate graphs for data sets. Fifth graders interchange, add, subtract, multiply, divide, order, and compare fractions (like and unlike denominators), mixed numbers, decimals, and percents. They understand probability (fractions or decimals 0 to 1). They solve range, mode, outliers, median, and mean for a set of data. Fifth graders measure area, perimeter, and volume, as well as angles (classify). They understand the circumference of a circle (diameter, radius), work with prime factorization (factors, exponents), and measure length, weight, volume, and temperature. They convert between the metric and U.S. customary systems.

Social Studies

Fifth graders study United States history to the late 1800s: Native Americans, settlers, early explorers, historical figures. They learn about life during the colonial era and its influence. The Revolutionary War, Declaration of Independence, and United States Constitution are studied, as well as slavery, geography, the Civil War, United States government, and the 50 states and their capitals. Fifth graders spend significant time learning about their personal heritage.

Science

Fifth graders study sound (transmission, applications) and light (characteristics, behavior). They learn more about the solar system (planets, earth, sun, moon) and about matter (atoms, elements, molecules) and its chemical and physical properties. They gain more in-depth knowledge about plants vs. animals (respiration and photosynthesis vs. digestion), carbon dioxide and oxygen, and the roles and cycles of plants and animals. Cells are introduced in terms of basic functions. Fifth graders learn more about the water cycle (evaporation, condensation, precipitation, etc.), the ocean environment (physical, biological), and rocks and minerals (classifications).

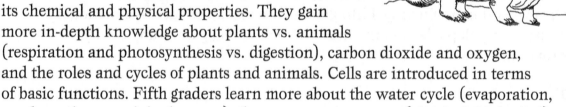

Sixth Grade (11-12 Years Old)
Who

Sixth graders are beginning to go through physical and emotional changes that can cause mood swings. This can lead to distraction from their work. At times, their social life can take priority over their academic life, and they enjoy time away from adults. They are very conscious of what their peers think of them, despite having a stronger sense of self. Peer approval is very important to them. They are aware of societal trends and care about having the very latest material possessions. They enjoy humor, discussing deep topics, and exploring issues and their role in the world.

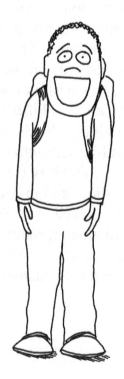

What

Reading

Sixth graders are working toward reading 150 words per minute. They read more in-depth text for a purpose and to engage in rich discussions. Chapter books (fiction, nonfiction), informational texts, and poetry are a part of their reading repertoire. They can better interpret meaning, literary devices, relationships, and conclusions, and they can spot inconsistencies and propaganda in what they are asked to read. Poetry gets more complex at this stage, and students learn more about style, tone, and meaning (structure, implied meaning, and imagery). Sixth graders do online research and use a variety of reference data to develop their ideas about the world.

Writing

Sixth graders continue to use the writing process to produce multiparagraph essays (persuasive, expository, narrative), letters, reports, and responses to literature. They write with purpose, tone, and a clear point of view or voice, and they take their audience into account. They use, compile, and interpret research material and decide what will be most meaningful to draw from. They focus on grammar, writing conventions, spelling, details, and voice in their essays.

Math

Sixth graders continue with decimals, fractions, and percents. They plot decimals, fractions, mixed numbers, and integers on a number line. They learn more about probability, rates, ratios, and proportions. They master the critical concepts of adding, subtracting, multiplying, and dividing fractions, mixed numbers, and integers. They study mean, median, mode, range, and outliers for a data set, and organizing and interpreting data with a variety of graphical methods. Prime factorization, the greatest common factor (GCF), and the least common multiple (LCM) of a pair of numbers are solidified, as are exponents, order of operations, area, perimeter, and volume of shapes, solids, and circles (area, circumference). They classify and measure angles. They understand congruent and noncongruent figures. They solve multistep problems. They measure, compare, and convert units of measure (metric and U.S. customary). They solve for a variable.

$3 + 2 = 5$

Social Studies

Sixth graders study world history from the late 1800s to the present, including economic, social, and religious aspects. The ancient civilizations of Mesopotamia, Egypt, Kush, the ancient Hebrews, Greece, the Persian Empire, India, China, and Rome are discussed, as are the rise and fall of these civilizations. The effects of wars on the American woman's role in history are examined.

Science

Sixth graders study the planet Earth, including its structure, layers, and plate tectonics. Major events with mountain and land formations, volcanoes, earthquakes, and glaciers are examined. They study the weather, water systems and cycles, natural resources, conservation, renewable vs. nonrenewable energy, erosion, and deposition. They learn about forms of energy (kinetic, potential) and transfer (conduction, radiation, convection). Sixth graders study weather patterns and causes, convection currents in both the oceans and the atmosphere, and ecosystems and the role of organisms within an ecosystem. States of matter (solid, liquid, gas), ecology, conservation, and the debate about climate change and/or global warming are studied.

Understanding the Curriculum

How are the curricular areas subdivided? What tools are useful for each curricular area? These two very important questions involve understanding the curriculum and how it is set up. In this section, each curricular area is broken down into subcategories. Knowing these categories will help you comprehend your grade-level curriculum requirements. Here you will find an overview of the major parts of each subject area of the curriculum, but you will need to refer to national and state standards for specifics.

Language Arts: Reading

This section suggests several ways you can incorporate reading comprehension strategies into your curriculum planning, the different ways you can have students read, and the reading genres that will enhance your students' interest in books. These ideas will help you build a comprehensive language arts program. The **Skill Tracker: Language Arts** and **Skill Tracker: Reading** templates can be used for this purpose.

32
Skill Tracker: Language Arts
35
Skill Tracker: Reading
03
Bookmarks

Comprehension Strategies

To assist students with comprehension, the **Bookmarks** template can be used.

- Author's point of view
  - Who is telling the story?
  - First person: I, me, my
  - Third person: he/she/they, him/her/them, his/hers/theirs
- Author's purpose
  - To entertain
  - To explain
  - To inform
  - To persuade

- Main ideas and details
  - What is the primary focus of the story?
  - What are the setting and supporting events?
  - Who are the characters?
- Compare and contrast
  - Find similarities and differences.
  - What do the characters have in common? What makes them different?
- Cause and effect
  - What took place? (problem)
  - What were the outcomes? (solution)
- Classify and/or categorize
  - Sort story elements into similar groups.
- Opinion and fact
  - Feeling vs. real
  - Perspective: personal view vs. the reality of something

- Make connections
  - Relate the story to a personal experience.
  - Connect to the characters through shared commonalities.

Ways to Read

- Choral reading
  - Students read together in "unison reading."
  - Opportunities for repeated readings of a selected piece
  - Practice for oral reading
  - Excellent for poetry and rhymes
  - Repeated readings of big books

- Shared reading
  - Teacher reads big book or text and tracks words.
  - Students view and/or follow.
  - Develops phonemic awareness
  - Models reading fluency
- Independent reading
  - Students read independently.
  - Students practice learned strategies.
  - Builds fluency
  - Problem-solving application

- Sustained silent reading (SSR)
  - Students read silently to themselves.
  - Independent activity
  - Individual instructional level
  - Encourages reading by letting students choose something they want to read
- Guided reading
  - Teacher and students read book or text together.
  - Read-think-talk through the text
  - Supports intervention
  - Can also "echo read" (teacher reads and students reread)

- Read-aloud
    - Teacher reads to the class.
    - Class discussion can follow.
    - May include a follow-up activity (journals, art, and so on)
    - Pure enjoyment (students just listen)
- Popcorn reading
    - Teacher asks a willing student to begin reading aloud.
    - When the student stops, another student continues to read, without the teacher's direction.
    - Process continues until all students have read a portion.
    - Builds responsibility to participate
    - Lower-grade students can select the next reader from those who have not read yet.

- Timed reading
    - Students read for a designated number of minutes.
    - Student reads twice, attempting to read further the second time.
    - Number of words per minute is recorded.
    - Builds fluency

- Partner reading
    - Students pair up and take turns reading, helping one another.
    - Select a special place in the room to read.
    - Can pair students of different ability (high with medium, medium with low) or allow students to select a partner
    - Allows students to showcase their skills

- Buddy reading
    - A lower-grade student pairs with an upper-grade student.
    - Discuss a story after it's been read
    - Take turns reading aloud
    - Older student serves as a coach and/or reading mentor.

Reading Genres

- Realistic fiction
  - Takes place in modern times (here and now)
  - Features realistic plots and events
  - Characters are typically ordinary people with everyday problems.
- Nonfiction
  - True facts
  - Can be about any subject
- Biography
  - The story of a person's life told by another person

- Autobiography
  - The story of a person's life told by himself or herself
- Mystery
  - The plot features mysterious events, possibly supernatural.
  - The solution is explained or revealed by the end of the story.
  - Suspenseful
- Poetry
  - Verse, frequently with rhythm or a specific rhyme scheme
  - Can feature closed or open patterns
  - Gives rise to thoughts and feelings
- Science fiction
  - Blends scientific fact and fiction to create a story
  - Can incorporate futuristic technology and fantastical scenarios
- Folktale
  - The original author is not always known, as stories are passed from generation to generation.
  - Could be a legend
- Myth
  - Explains a natural phenomenon, belief, or practice
  - Gods and/or superhumans
- Drama
  - Written to act out
  - Usually has an audience

Language Arts: Writing

In this section, we review the various writing styles and the genres related to writing instruction. This will help you build a comprehensive language arts program. The **Skill Tracker: Language Arts** and **Skill Tracker: Writing** templates can be used for this purpose.

The Writing Process

The **Writing Process Folder** and **Writing Process Tracker** templates can be used to assist you with the management of student writing.

- **Pre-write**—Students brainstorm ideas on paper, using graphic organizers.
- **Draft**—Students write down their thoughts, take notes on the main idea and details, and remember that this should be "no worry" writing.
- **Edit/Revise**—Students check for clarity and content, add or change information, look for needed details.
- **Proofread**—Students check for grammar and spelling errors and review mechanics.
- **Publish**—Students create the final draft. This should be the best version.
- **Share/Reflect**—Students share their work with the class, discuss one another's writing, and have work displayed on bulletin boards.

Types of Writing Styles

- **Independent writing**—Students write independently through a variety of forms (journals, labeling, student books, personal essays, and so on).
- **Interactive writing**—The teacher and students plan and write a class story as a group, taking turns, modeling, and supporting one another's ideas.
- **Shared writing**—The teacher writes as the students compose, copy, and/or transcribe.
- **Guided writing** (also called writer's workshop)—The teacher works with a small group, and they write together as a community of writers.

Writing Genres

- **Narrative writing**—Tells a story, gives an account, uses imagination or personal accounts. This can be written in the first person (using "I" or "we" as the narrator) or third person (using "he," "she," "it," or "they").
- **Expository writing**—Explains or defines; gives information; uses facts, statistical information, cause and effect, and examples. Always written in the third person.
- **Descriptive writing**—Shows, not just tells, by describing something, using descriptive language and adjectives. Can be written in the first or third person.
- **Summary writing**—Summarizes, while maintaining the integrity of the original document. Uses main ideas, events, and concepts. Can be written in the first or third person.
- **Response to literature**—Reacts or responds to literature, using a personal connection to a writer's ideas or experiences. This form uses meaning, is written largely by retelling, summarizing, analyzing, and/or generalizing.
- **Poetry writing**—Arranged composition, uses sound and/or rhythm. There are many types of poetry, including concrete, lyric, narrative, closed verse, haiku, cinquain, limericks, and nonsense verse.
- **Report writing**—Explains and informs, gives information and facts, requires research. This style of writing is used to educate, report facts, and make predictions based on data.
- **Friendly letter writing**—To create friendly, formal, or business correspondence, to convey or share information. A letter requires elements such as the date, a greeting, one or more body paragraphs, a closing, and a signature.

Tips and Tools for the Writing Teacher

- Use pictures for writing prompts. Get these from old calendars, magazines, newspapers, personal photos, and so on.
- Use graphic organizers to get ideas flowing.
- Have students use Word, PowerPoint, Pages, or Keynote. Technology is your friend.
- Have plenty of paper on hand—lined, copy, construction, or butcher paper.

Suggested Literacy Websites

- http://pbskids.org/lions/
- http://www.bbc.co.uk/schools/typing/
- http://www.bookpop.com/index2.html
- http://www.icdlbooks.org
- http://www.mightybook.com/
- http://www.readprint.com/
- http://www.saskschools.ca/~ebooks/
- http://www.starfall.com
- http://www.storylineonline.net/
- http://www.tumblebooks.com

Math

Mathematics is taught sequentially, aligning to the developmentally age-appropriate skills and concepts of the students. In other words, students are introduced to skills that they are ready for and that lay the foundation for higher-level skills to be introduced consecutively in subsequent grade levels. Following is an overview of the basic math strands taught throughout the year. Since the math curriculum can vary from state to state, consult your state standards and your state or district's adopted curriculum. The **Skill Tracker: Math** template can be used for this purpose.

33
Skill Tracker:
Math

Number Sense

Number sense involves gaining an understanding of numbers, their relationships, and what they represent. This comprises the majority of the math curriculum. Number sense includes everything from counting and place value to factoring and operations. The **Math Fact Fruit Plate** template can be used to track student mastery of math facts. Some of the components may include:

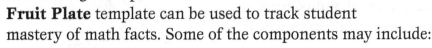

23
Math Fact
Fruit Plate

- Counting
- Patterns
- Operations ($+$, $-$, $\times$, $\div$)
- Place value
- Money
- Fractions
- Decimals
- Percents
- Factoring
- Integers

Teaching Tips and Tools for Number Sense

- Use manipulatives to build number sense through hands-on experiences.
- Use number lines.
- Use a 100s chart.
- Use flash cards.
- Use counting and counting patterns (for example, one more/one less, ten more/ten less).
- Use counting on and counting back for addition and subtraction.

Measurement and Geometry

Measurement involves length, volume, weight, and time. Geometry involves shapes and solids, their characteristics, and their area and perimeter. Some of the components may include:

- Clocks
- Calendars
- Geometric shapes, forms, and solids
- Polygons, including quadrilaterals
- Angles
- Triangles
- Perimeter, area, circumference, and volume
- Rulers (metric or U.S. customary)
- Units of measure conversions
- Grids and plotting

Teaching Tips and Tools for Measurement and Geometry

- Use wooden or plastic solids and shapes as tangible tools.
- Measure items in the classroom as a good way to solidify concepts using articles the students are familiar with.
- Set up a center for measurement and volume.
- Use calendar activities, incorporating money, tallies, and place value.

Algebra

Algebra involves solving mathematical problems through interpretations and properties. Some of the components may include:

- Classifying and sorting
- Story problems
- Operational symbols
- Properties of equality
- Solving equations
- Solving for a variable
- Solving problems with graphs and tables

Teaching Tips and Tools for Algebra

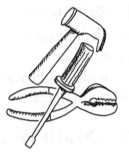

- Use a "problem of the day" with the whole class.
- Use math journals to solve and explain problems.
- Incorporate current events to discuss and solve.

Statistics, Data Analysis, and Probability

Statistics, data analysis, and probability involve analyzing, comparing, predicting, and interpreting data. Some of the components may include:

- Patterning
- Graphing
- Tally charts
- Mean, median, mode, range
- Outcomes and probability
- Line plots and coordinates
- Comparing data sets
- Fractions and percents

Teaching Tips and Tools for Statistics, Data Analysis, and Probability

- Use manipulatives with graphing grids and mats.
- Use coin tosses, dice rolls, or pulling M&Ms out of an opaque bag.
- Calculate percentages using M&Ms, Skittles, or counters.
- Graph birthdays with a pictograph.

Mathematical Reasoning

Mathematical reasoning explains the approach to a problem and its solution, as well as its application to other problems. Some of the components may include:

- Using tools to solve a problem
- Estimating
- Sequencing and prioritizing information
- Explaining strategies used and why

Teaching Tips and Tools for Mathematical Reasoning

- Use a "problem of the day" with the whole class.
- Use story problems.
- Present real-life applications.
- Write about problems in math journals.

Suggested Math Websites

- http://www.aaamath.com/
- http://www.coolmath.com/
- http://www.coolmath4kids.com/
- http://www.figurethis.org/index.html
- http://www.ixl.com/
- http://www.math.harvard.edu/~knill/mathmovies/
- http://www.mathcats.com/
- http://www.mathforum.com/

Social Studies

Social studies is the study of our world, its people, and their interactions with one another. Studying these connections and relationships gives students an understanding of their place in their school, as well as their role in their community, their state, their country, and in the world. There are many elements introduced over the course of a student's school years. Though several of these elements overlap, they are introduced at age-appropriate levels of understanding.

The **Skill Tracker: Social Studies** template can be used for this purpose. Your curriculum and state standards will guide you, but here is a list of topics you will study, depending on grade level:

37
Skill Tracker:
Social Studies

- Careers
- Present vs. past
- National symbols, icons, and traditions
- Commerce

- Cultural diversity
- United States history
- Ancient history
- Causes and effects of war
- Folklore
- Heroes
- Economics
- Maps and globes
- Citizenship
- Government
- Community
- Holidays
- Character
- Conflict resolution and communication

Teaching Tips and Tools for Social Studies

You may want to include the following components:

- Timelines
- Children's and young adults' historical fiction books
- Children's and young adults' nonfiction books
- Internet research
- Pictures
- Cultural artifacts
- Videos and DVDs
- Social studies journals
- Minibooks
- Research report outlines
- Primary resources
- Maps—topographical and two-dimensional
- Guest speakers
- Field trips
- Posters

Suggested Social Studies Websites

- http://www.50states.com/
- http://www.edhelper.com/Social_Studies.htm
- http://www.freerice.com/
- http://www.pbs.org/teachers/socialstudies/
- http://www.proteacher.com/090000.shtml
- http://www.socialstudiesforkids.com/
- http://www.teachwithmovies.org/

Science

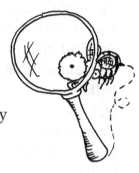

Science comprises three major strands. Each grade level generally involves instruction in all three strands. Learning at one grade level lays the foundation for subsequent learning in later grades. While certain areas of science instruction may appeal to you more than others, it is important that your primary goal be to teach what is addressed in your state standards; this ensures students' preparedness for the next year. The **Skill Tracker: Science** template can be used for this purpose.

36
Skill Tracker:
Science

Life Science

Life science is the study of everything pertaining to life. Following is a general list of life science topics. Check grade-level state standards and curriculum guides for specifics.

- Plants
- Food chain
- Herbivores
- Carnivores
- Insects and spiders
- Ocean life
- Amphibians
- Fish
- Dinosaurs
- Birds
- Mammals
- Humans, including the human body
- The five senses

Physical Science

Physical science is the study of physical phenomena in nature. Following is a general list of physical science topics that may be covered at your grade level. Check your state's grade-level standards for specifics.

- Energy and matter
- Sound
- Electricity
- Light
- Magnets
- Simple machines
- Shadows

Earth Science

Earth science focuses on Earth and its physical structures, cycles, and relationships. Space science falls under this strand as it relates to Earth as a planet. Following is a general list of earth science topics that may be covered at your grade level. Check grade-level standards for your state.

- Land forms
- Geology (rocks)
- Air
- Water, including the water cycle
- Habitats
- Recycling
- Endangered species
- Solar system and planets
- Sun and moon
- Seasons
- Weather, including clouds

Teaching Tips and Tools for Science

You may want to include the following components:

- Children's and young adults' nonfiction books
- Internet research
- Pictures
- Videos and DVDs
- Research report outlines
- Artifacts from a natural history museum
- Field trip to a natural history museum
- Maps—topographical and two-dimensional
- Guest speakers
- Minibooks
- Science journals
- Science kits (for example, Full Option Science System (FOSS))
- Posters
- Experiments

Suggested Science Websites

- http://kids.mtpe.hq.nasa.gov/
- http://kids.nationalgeographic.com/kids/
- http://school.discoveryeducation.com/index.html
- http://www.chem4kids.com/
- http://www.hhmi.org/coolscience/

Physical Education

General classroom teachers may find it intimidating to plan and deliver instruction in physical education as a subject area. While most teachers are active and work out on their own, they don't have the formal training to deliver organized P.E. instruction. Knowing the state content standards for your grade level will help you establish learning goals and objectives for physical education. The **Skill Tracker: P.E.** template can be used for this purpose.

34
Skill Tracker:
P.E.

Consider implementing a sequential, appropriate curriculum to help students acquire the knowledge, skills, attitudes, and confidence needed to adopt and maintain a physically active, healthy lifestyle. Check with your school and/or district to see if there is an available curriculum guide. Following are concepts that are consistent in all grade levels, but expand through the years. Consult the state content standards for your grade level.

- **Aerobic capacity**—Understand the connection between heart, lungs, muscles, blood, and oxygen during physical activity.
- **Assessment**—Perform at age-appropriate standards for aerobic capacity, muscular strength, flexibility, and body composition, using a health-related fitness assessment.
- **Body composition**—Participate in physical activity for increasing time periods; understand the body.
- **Body management**—Balance different elements; maintain personal space.
- **Fitness concepts**—Participate on a consistent basis, including warm-up and cool-down; understand intensity and duration.
- **Flexibility**—Stretch muscles for specified periods of time.
- **Group dynamics**—Participate cooperatively with others, participate in teamwork.
- **Locomotor movement**—Walk, run, slide, jump, perform other plyometric exercises and activities.
- **Manipulative skills**—Balance, roll, throw, catch, kick, strike, hand and foot dribble, punt, hit, pass, volley.
- **Movement concepts**—Develop range and efficiency by teaching and reteaching skill themes in various ways.
- **Muscular strength and/or endurance**—Perform abs, push-ups, lunges, squats.
- **Rhythmic skills**—Dance, learn rhythm with connections to music and/or a beat.
- **Self-responsibility**—Participate in a group and be responsible for oneself.
- **Social interaction**—Encourage others, problem-solve, respect one another and the equipment.

Teaching Tips and Tools for Physical Education

You may want to include the following equipment:

- Cones (for interval training and dribble and/or kicking practice)
- Soccer nets
- Variety of athletic balls (basketball, soccer ball, handball)
- Hula-Hoops
- Beanbags (for hopscotch)
- Jump ropes
- Tetherball court and ball
- Volleyball and net

You may also want to include the following components:

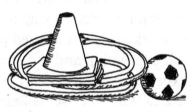

- Research about the Olympics
- Research about well-known athletes
- Guest speakers (athletes)
- Physical education journals (record workouts, times, goals)

Suggested Physical Education Websites

- http://pecentral.com/
- http://www.peoffice.co.uk/
- http://www.physicaleducationupdate.com/

Visual and Performing Arts

The visual and performing arts are a critical part of a well-rounded curriculum for all students, even though they are often left out of the daily elementary curriculum. Dance, music, theater, and the visual arts span all cultures, ages, and interests. The arts encourage creativity and imagination. They give students the opportunity to try new things, work collaboratively, and apply self-discipline.

Typically, the visual and performing arts curriculum includes abilities in dance, music, theater, and the visual arts that all students should be able to master at specific grade levels, if given the opportunity to practice. The **Skill Tracker: Arts** template can be used for this purpose.

28
Skill Tracker:
Arts

The visual and performing arts curriculum may be grouped under the following five strands. Check your state standards for specifics.

- Artistic perception
- Creative expression
- Historical and cultural context
- Aesthetic values
- Connections, relations, and applications

At each grade level, more specific learning is delivered for each strand.

Review the content standards for previous grade levels for help in planning lessons that build on past experiences for each of the strands, especially if your own experience offers little in the way of training for this area. A thoughtful curriculum design provides students with alternative ways to perceive and experience the world. A standards-based arts education program provides a way for all students to work at a personalized pace, develop self-expression and self-confidence, and experience a sense of accomplishment. Check with your school and/or district to see if there is an available curriculum guide to use for planning and instruction.

Teaching Tips and Tools for Visual and Performing Arts

In order for students to excel in the arts, they need opportunities to develop skills through a comprehensive education in the arts. You may want to include the following components:

- Practice time
- Rehearsal time
- Reading about the arts and artists
- Researching, writing, and communicating about the arts
- Reflecting on the arts through journal writing about one's observations, feelings, and ideas about the arts
- Participating in art critiques
- Making connections between the arts and other curricular subject areas
- Connecting the arts disciplines (dance, music, theater, and the visual arts)
- Pictures
- Field trips to productions and museums
- Guest speakers
- Videos
- Internet research

Suggested Visual and Performing Arts Websites

- http://techyteacher.net/
- http://www.getty.edu/education/teachers/index.html
- http://www.khake.com/page87.html
- http://www.kinderart.com/
- http://www.kodak.com/global/en/consumer/education/lessonPlans/indices/art.shtml
- http://www.moma.org/interactives/destination/
- http://www.princetonol.com/groups/iad/

Cross-Curricular Subject Areas

In addition to the specific subject areas discussed above, Health, Geography, and English Language Development (E.L.D.) are linked through several curricular areas. Some districts designate a block of time, adopted curriculum series, and/or formal and organized assessment for these subject areas.

Health

Health awareness should be an integral part of the classroom experience. Every time your students are up and moving and stretching, they are learning the importance of movement. Every time your students go to P.E., they learn the importance of exercise. Every time you validate your students' hard work, you are boosting their emotional needs. When you teach a cooking lesson, your students watch what you put into the recipe and your use of math in measuring. Every time they have a snack, they can be learning which snacks are healthy and which are not. Health is a constant in every school day. You can also plan specific lessons in the subject. The **Skill Tracker: Health** template can be used for this purpose.

31
Skill Tracker:
Health

Geography

Geography can easily be adapted to many curricular areas. The use of maps in social studies supports this. When you read a multicultural book aloud and show students where the story comes from on the world map, you are linking reading and geography. When you discuss space in the classroom, at the school, and within the community, you are teaching students about geography. You will likely plan lessons dedicated specifically to geographic regions, but geography can be a part of the curriculum all the time in organic ways. The **Skill Tracker: Geography** template can be used for this purpose.

30
Skill Tracker:
Geography

English Language Development

Students in English Language Development (E.L.D.) programs have a separate class in English. However, English is also taught in every curricular area. Labeling, modeling, repeating, grouping, partnering, and discussing are included in every subject area and should be considered when planning every lesson. The **Skill Tracker: E.L.D.** template can be used for this purpose.

29
Skill Tracker:
E.L.D.

Curriculum Planning

When planning for all subject areas, it's important to know your students' knowledge base and needs. Pre-assessments, post-assessments, student surveys, and teacher- and/or student-led conferences will help you know what to include in your planning, how to structure small groups, and what curriculum needs to be introduced. You teach more and allow for more skill-based learning when you link across curricular areas. Use the skill tracker templates for Arts, E.L.D., Geography, Health, Language Arts, Math, P.E., Reading, Science, Social Studies, and Writing to note student progress.

Templates

The key on pages 248–251 lists the templates available as PDFs on the accompanying CD. The key includes the number of each template, as well as information and instructions for its use. The symbol ⌨ next to a template number in the key indicates that the template is also available as a PDF electronic form, which can be filled in on a computer and printed. Adobe Reader is required to open PDFs.

Thumbnails of all templates are reproduced on pages 252–272. The symbol ⌨ after a template number on the thumbnail pages has the same meaning as in the key below.

Be sure to set Adobe Reader to highlight the form fields as follows:

    Preferences >
    Forms >
    Highlight Color: ☑ Show border hover color for fields

Note that your filled-in forms cannot be saved on the computer.

A gray arrow at the side edge of a template (for example, ▬) indicates that the template is included with an adjoining template in a multipage PDF.

🖳 **01 Anecdotal Log**

Use this log to record detailed observations of student behavior. Save the log as formal documentation for referral procedures and parent/guardian conferences.

🖳 **02 Assessment Portfolio**

Use this log to track students' summative and formative assessments. Save the log as formal documentation for preparing progress reports and report cards, as well as for accessing during parent/guardian conferences.

03 Bookmarks

Cut out each bookmark along the outer edge. Fold on the dashed line and glue the halves together, or cut in half on the dashed line in order to make two different bookmarks. Encourage students to use the bookmarks when reading.

🖳 **04 Bulletin Board Labels**

Use these labels for the title (or heading) of your bulletin board.

05 Bulletin Board Planner

Sketch out your bulletin board. Plan your rubric. Create a title and an open-ended question to place on the bulletin board. Write applicable state standards or learning objectives using student-friendly language.

06 Center Sign-In Sheet

Use this sign-in sheet to track students' use of an individual learning center.

🖳 **07 Center Tracker**

Fill in the name of each classroom learning center. Use this roster to track student participation at the learning centers.

08 Classroom Map

Cut out the classroom furniture and other elements on the second and third pages; use them with the classroom outline on the first page to arrange your classroom.

09 Comments and Suggestions Slips

Students record their comments or suggestions on the forms and place them in a Comment/Suggestion Box. These can be discussed as a class.

10 Conflict Resolution Slips

Copy these forms and make them available to your students. Students work together to discuss and resolve their conflict, then submit the completed slips to the teacher and share the resolution they have decided on.

🖳 **11 Debate Organizer**

Use this form to organize debate teams and develop questions for them to debate.
Optional: Use Student Question forms to generate questions as a whole class activity.

🖳 **12 Desk Name Tag**

Have students print, write, or type their name in the center panel. Students can decorate their name tag. The name tags can then be folded along the dotted lines, tucking the bottom section underneath to create a name tag that stands by itself.

🖳 **13 Equipment Inventory**

Record all equipment (computers, overhead projectors, etc.) on this inventory sheet. Keep a copy to file for the end-of-year school inventory.

14 Group Investigation

Use this form to organize small groups of students who will research a topic and report their findings.

15 "I Am" Poem Planner

Students use this organizer to create their poem.

16 "I Come From" Poem Planner

Students use this organizer to plan their poem.

17 Incident Reports

Use this form to document any incident for which you may need written documentation concerning the incident itself, who was present, what was done, and follow-up.

18 Jigsaw Organizer

Students write section headings or questions inside the circle, then take notes in each square.

19 Lesson Plan: Open-Ended

Available with instructions and without instructions.

20 Lesson Plan: Direct Instruction

Available with instructions and without instructions.

21 Lesson Plan: Into-Through-and-Beyond

Available with instructions and without instructions.

22 Library Labels

Use these labels to categorize the books in your classroom library. Labels can be attached to shelves or containers that hold the corresponding category of books.

23 Math Fact Fruit Plate

A paper plate is needed for this activity. Students write the numbers 1 through 12 on the pieces of fruit, including the math sign (+, −, ×, ÷) for the current unit, then cut out the pieces of fruit. Starting with the "1" fruit, students glue each piece of fruit to the plate as they master the math facts for that number.

24 Must Do/May Do

Complete each form with up to five Must Do and May Do activities. Post these lists for your students.

25 Procedures Log

Use this log to record your classroom procedures. Have it available for a substitute teacher, to send home to parents, or to provide to an administrator.

26 Rule Planner

Write the rule under consideration, and describe the situation that causes you to consider this rule. Describe the effect the rule will have. What will result from having this rule?

27 Scavenger Hunt Questionnaire

Ask students in your class to complete the questionnaire. Each student's name can be written down only one time.

28 Skill Tracker: Arts

Fill in the name of each skill or standard to be documented. Use this roster to track student achievement in the Arts.

🖥 **29** Skill Tracker: E.L.D.

Fill in the name of each skill or standard to be documented. Use this roster to track student achievement in English Language Development (E.L.D.) activities.

🖥 **30** Skill Tracker: Geography

Fill in the name of each skill or standard to be documented. Use this roster to track student achievement in Geography.

🖥 **31** Skill Tracker: Health

Fill in the name of each skill or standard to be documented. Use this roster to track student achievement in Health.

🖥 **32** Skill Tracker: Language Arts

Fill in the name of each skill or standard to be documented. Use this roster to track student achievement in Language Arts.

🖥 **33** Skill Tracker: Math

Fill in the name of each skill or standard to be documented. Use this roster to track student achievement in Math.

🖥 **34** Skill Tracker: P.E.

Fill in the name of each skill or standard to be documented. Use this roster to track student achievement in Physical Education (P.E.).

🖥 **35** Skill Tracker: Reading

Fill in the name of each skill or standard to be documented. Use this roster to track student achievement in Reading.

🖥 **36** Skill Tracker: Science

Fill in the name of each skill or standard to be documented. Use this roster to track student achievement in Science.

🖥 **37** Skill Tracker: Social Studies

Fill in the name of each skill or standard to be documented. Use this roster to track student achievement in Social Studies.

🖥 **38** Skill Tracker: Writing

Fill in the name of each skill or standard to be documented. Use this roster to track student achievement in Writing.

🖥 **39** Student Contact Information

Complete the form with contact information for each student in your class.

40 Student Interest Survey

Students complete this survey about themselves.

🖥 **41** Student Name Cards

Record each student's name on a card, then print them out on card stock. Use the cards to call on students randomly in class.

🖥 **42** Student Name Strips

Record each student's name on a strip, then print them out on card stock. Use the strips to call on students randomly in class.

43 Student Portfolio

Students record each assignment selected for their student portfolio and explain why it was chosen. They write down what they learned from that assignment.

44 Student Question Forms

Write key words or skills from the current unit on the top section, and attach it to the outside of a manila envelope. Students write their question or problem on a Student Question form and write their answer on the back. They place their form in the envelope and pass it to the next student.

45 Student Response Forms

Write a question about a learned or will-learn activity on the top section, and attach it to the outside of a manila envelope. Students write their responses on a Student Response form. They place their form in the envelope and pass it to the next student.

46 Textbook Inventory

Use this inventory sheet to track all textbooks, teacher's editions, resource kits, etc., that have been assigned to your classroom. Keep a copy to file for the end-of-year school inventory.

47 Textbook Sign-Out Sheet

Use this sign-out sheet to track textbooks assigned to students for the school year.

48 Time Capsule

Students complete the information on this cover sheet and attach it to the front of a manila envelope. They place all items inside the envelope and seal it, and the time capsule is stored until it is time for it to be opened.

49 Weekly Progress Reports

Complete a progress report for each student and send it home at the end of the week, to be returned with the parent's signature.

50 Writing Process Folder

Students decorate this cover page and glue it to a folder. Students track the writing process by using a paperclip attached to the side of the folder, moving it to align with the stage currently being worked on. Ongoing writing pages are kept in the folder. Students record the title of the writing assignment, the genre, and the date of the published work upon completion.

51 Writing Process Tracker

Students use these divider sheets to identify the different stages or versions of their writing project.

Anecdotal Log

Student _____ Date of birth _____

Teacher _____ Grade _____ Room _____

General comments/observations (behavior, grades, attitude, motivation, etc.)

Date _____ Time _____ Initials _____
Account/Observation

Date _____ Time _____ Initials _____
Account/Observation

Date _____ Time _____ Initials _____
Account/Observation

Date _____ Time _____ Initials _____
Account/Observation

Date _____ Time _____ Initials _____
Account/Observation

The Organized Teacher's Guide to Classroom Management — Anecdotal Log — CD 01   © The McGraw-Hill Companies, Inc.

01 🖥
Anecdotal Log

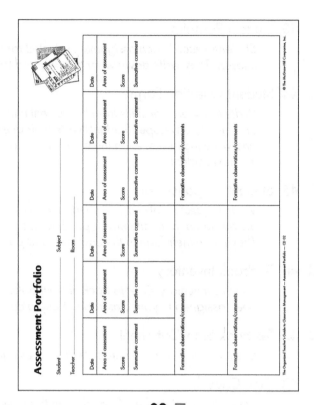

02 🖥
Assessment Portfolio

03
Bookmarks

04
Bulletin Board Labels

04

Bulletin Board Labels

04

Bulletin Board Labels

04 🖥

Bulletin Board Labels

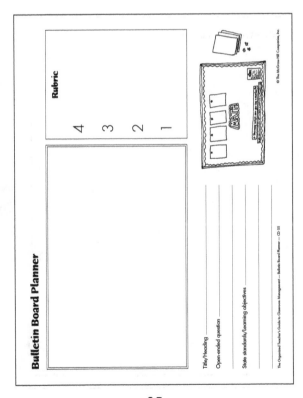

05

Bulletin Board Planner

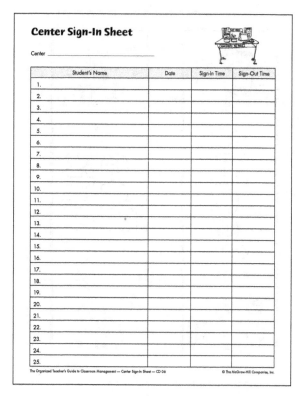

06
Center Sign-In Sheet

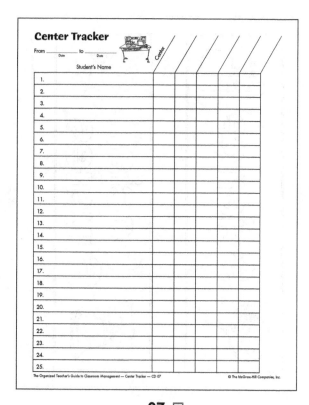

07 ⌨
Center Tracker

08
Classroom Map

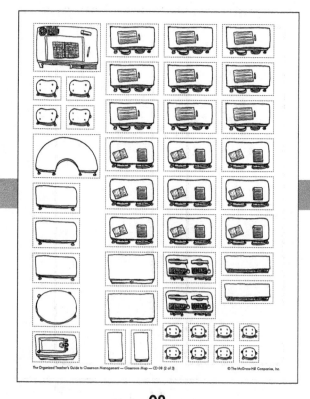

08
Classroom Map

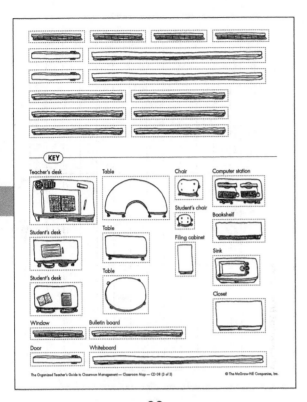

08

Classroom Map

Comments and Suggestions

Write your comment or suggestion on this slip and place it in the Comment/Suggestion Box.

Date _____ Location _____

I would like to make the following ☐ comment ☐ suggestion:

_____

_____

_____

Name (optional) _____

Comments and Suggestions

Write your comment or suggestion on this slip and place it in the Comment/Suggestion Box.

Date _____ Location _____

I would like to make the following ☐ comment ☐ suggestion:

_____

_____

_____

Name (optional) _____

Comments and Suggestions

Write your comment or suggestion on this slip and place it in the Comment/Suggestion Box.

Date _____ Location _____

I would like to make the following ☐ comment ☐ suggestion:

_____

_____

_____

Name (optional) _____

The Organized Teacher's Guide to Classroom Management — Comments and Suggestions Slips — CD 09   © The McGraw-Hill Companies, Inc.

09

Comments and Suggestions Slips

Conflict Resolution Slip   Date _____

Student 1 _____   Student 2 _____

Statement of the conflict _____

_____

Resolution checklist

☐ Discuss how the conflict makes you feel.
☐ Imagine how the other student feels.
☐ Discuss a resolution.
☐ Fill out the slip and submit it to the teacher.

Our resolution _____

_____

_____

Conflict Resolution Slip   Date _____

Student 1 _____   Student 2 _____

Statement of the conflict _____

_____

Resolution checklist

☐ Discuss how the conflict makes you feel.
☐ Imagine how the other student feels.
☐ Discuss a resolution.
☐ Fill out the slip and submit it to the teacher.

Our resolution _____

_____

_____

The Organized Teacher's Guide to Classroom Management — Conflict Resolution Slips — CD 10   © The McGraw-Hill Companies, Inc.

10

Conflict Resolution Slips

Debate Organizer

Unit/Chapter _____

Date _____

Topic
_____

Team A	Team B
1. _____	1. _____
2. _____	2. _____
3. _____	3. _____
4. _____	4. _____

Debate Questions

1. _____
2. _____
3. _____
4. _____
5. _____
6. _____
7. _____
8. _____
9. _____
10. _____

The Organized Teacher's Guide to Classroom Management — Debate Organizer — CD 11   © The McGraw-Hill Companies, Inc.

11 💻

Debate Organizer

Desk Name Tag

_____
Name

Desk Name Tag

1. Print, write, or type your name in the center panel above.
2. Decorate your name tag.
3. Fold along the dotted lines, tucking this section underneath to create a name tag that stands by itself.

12 🖳
Desk Name Tag

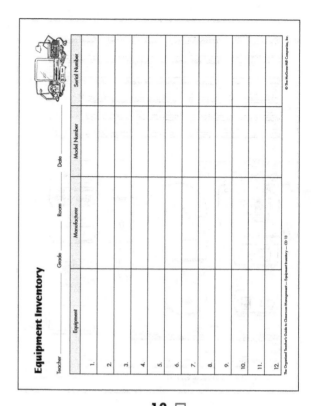

Equipment Inventory

Teacher	Grade	Room	Date
Equipment	Manufacturer	Model Number	Serial Number
1.			
2.			
3.			
4.			
5.			
6.			
7.			
8.			
9.			
10.			
11.			
12.			

13 🖳
Equipment Inventory

Group Investigation

Unit/Chapter _____
Date _____

Topic

Group Members

1. _____   5. _____
2. _____   6. _____
3. _____   7. _____
4. _____   8. _____

Source (text, article, website)
Notes/Findings

Source (text, article, website)
Notes/Findings

Source (text, article, website)
Notes/Findings

14 🖳
Group Investigation

"I Am" Poem Planner

Name _____   Date _____
Room _____   Period _____

Line 1   I am (two special qualities about yourself) _____ and _____
Line 2   I wonder (something you are curious about) _____
Line 3   I hear (an imaginary or actual sound) _____
Line 4   I see (an imaginary or actual sight) _____
Line 5   I want (something you desire) _____
Line 6   I am (repeat the first line of the poem) _____ and _____
Line 7   I pretend (something you could pretend to do) _____
Line 8   I feel (a feeling about something imaginary) _____
Line 9   I touch (something imaginary) _____
Line 10   I worry (something that really bothers or worries you) _____
Line 11   I cry (something that makes you sad) _____
Line 12   I am (repeat the first line of the poem) _____ and _____
Line 13   I understand (something you know well) _____
Line 14   I say (something you believe in) _____
Line 15   I dream (something you dream about) _____
Line 16   I try (something you make an effort to do) _____
Line 17   I hope (something you hope for) _____
Line 18   I am (repeat the first line of the poem) _____ and _____

15
"I Am" Poem Planner

"I Come From" Poem Planner

Name _____ Date _____

Room _____ Period _____

Describe a time in your childhood when you felt the happiest.
_____
_____

Describe a time or place in your childhood when/where you felt the safest.
_____
_____

Describe a time with a sibling, cousin, or other family member that made you laugh really hard,
and only the two of you understood why you were laughing. _____

Describe the place where you grew up (the city, your street, your house, etc.).
_____
_____

Describe your favorite season in detail and tell why you love it. _____

Describe your favorite food: the way it smells, when it tastes the best, and how it makes you feel.
_____
_____

Describe a time when you were sad, scared, or confused. _____

Describe a day that was so perfect you couldn't possibly imagine anything better.
_____
_____

Describe your favorite holiday/celebration spent with your family. _____

Incident Report

Date _____ Time _____ Location _____

Incident (What did the student do? What happened?)

Witnesses (Who was present?) 1. 2. 3.	**Initial response** (What did you do? What was done?)
Follow-up ☐ Office ☐ Referral to _____ (nurse/counselor/specialist) ☐ Home communication	**Follow-up feedback/Action plan**

Incident Report

Date _____ Time _____ Location _____

Incident (What did the student do? What happened?)

Witnesses (Who was present?) 1. 2. 3.	**Initial response** (What did you do? What was done?)
Follow-up ☐ Office ☐ Referral to _____ (nurse/counselor/specialist) ☐ Home communication	**Follow-up feedback/Action plan**

16
"I Come From" Poem Planner

17 💻
Incident Reports

Jigsaw Organizer

Name _____ Date _____

1. Write section headings or questions inside the circle.
2. Take notes in each square.

Lesson Plan: Open-Ended

Title _____

Unit _____ Grade level _____

Teacher _____ Total time _____

1. Anticipatory Set and Scaffolding   Allotted time _____
Explain how you will grab the students' attention.

Objective
State learning objectives: "By the end of the lesson, students will be able to . . ."

2. Presentation/Procedure   Allotted time _____
List the sequence of steps for the lesson. Include guided practice,
checking for understanding, and independent practice.

18
Jigsaw Organizer

19
Lesson Plan: Open-Ended
(with instructions)

---

3. Critical Thinking
Describe in terms of Bloom's Taxonomy, Gardner's Multiple Intelligences, learning styles, etc.

Allotted time _____

4. Assessment/Homework/Project
Assign work that will help students continue to master the objective.

Allotted time _____

5. State Content Standards
Note the state standards that are addressed in the lesson.

Allotted time _____

6. Modifications/Special Needs/Technology
Note modifications, differentiation of instruction, technology needs, use of an aide, etc.

Allotted time _____

19
Lesson Plan: Open-Ended
(with instructions)

Lesson Plan: Open-Ended

Title _____

Unit _____ Grade level _____

Teacher _____ Total time _____

1. Anticipatory Set and Scaffolding

Allotted time _____

Objective

2. Presentation/Procedure

Allotted time _____

19 💻
Lesson Plan: Open-Ended
(without instructions)

---

3. Critical Thinking

Allotted time _____

4. Assessment/Homework/Project

Allotted time _____

5. State Content Standards

Allotted time _____

6. Modifications/Special Needs/Technology

Allotted time _____

19 💻
Lesson Plan: Open-Ended
(without instructions)

Lesson Plan: Direct Instruction

Title _____

Unit _____ Grade level _____

Teacher _____ Suggested time _____

Instructional Objectives
State learning objectives: "By the end of the lesson, students will be able to . . ."

Materials and Equipment
Note required materials and equipment or technology needs.

Vocabulary
List new or unfamiliar vocabulary that will be addressed in the lesson.

Anticipatory Set
Explain how you will grab the students' attention.

Input
Note past information that is relevant to the lesson.

Lesson Steps
List the sequence of steps for the lesson.

20
Lesson Plan: Direct Instruction
(with instructions)

Guided Practice
Describe the activity that the students and teacher can perform together toward meeting the objective.

Check for Understanding
Do a quick and simple assessment to confirm student understanding.

Independent Practice
Have students work independently on a task in direct correlation with the objective.

Closure
Review what was learned during the lesson through a series of related questions or ideas.

State Content Standards
Note the state standards that are addressed in the lesson.

Modifications/Special Needs/Technology
Note modifications, differentiation of instruction, technology needs, use of an aide, etc.

Assessment/Homework/Project
Assign work that will help students continue to master the objective.

20
Lesson Plan: Direct Instruction
(with instructions)

Lesson Plan: Direct Instruction

Title _____

Unit _____   Grade level _____

Teacher _____   Suggested time _____

Instructional Objectives
Materials and Equipment
Vocabulary
Anticipatory Set
Input
Lesson Steps

20 💻
Lesson Plan: Direct Instruction
(without instructions)

Guided Practice
Check for Understanding
Independent Practice
Closure
State Content Standards
Modifications/Special Needs/Technology
Assessment/Homework/Project

20 💻
Lesson Plan: Direct Instruction
(without instructions)

Lesson Plan: Into-Through-and-Beyond

Think
What is the "big idea" you want students to be thinking about? What are the essential questions?

Objectives
What will students learn from this lesson? How will you measure mastery? "By the end of the lesson, students will be able to . . ."

State Content Standards
Note the state standards that are addressed in the lesson.

INTO
Provide initial activities that introduce your students to—or prepare them for—the concepts and skills to be covered in the lesson. Connect the "big idea" of the lesson to students' experiences.

THROUGH
What will you model for your students? What activities provide the context and content for learning?

21
Lesson Plan: Into-Through-and-Beyond
(with instructions)

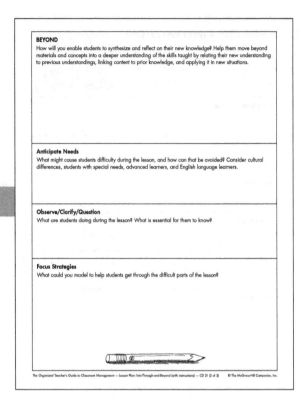

BEYOND
How will you enable students to synthesize and reflect on their new knowledge? Help them move beyond materials and concepts into a deeper understanding of the skills taught by relating their new understanding to previous understandings, linking content to prior knowledge, and applying it in new situations.

Anticipate Needs
What might cause students difficulty during the lesson, and how can that be avoided? Consider cultural differences, students with special needs, advanced learners, and English language learners.

Observe/Clarify/Question
What are students doing during the lesson? What is essential for them to know?

Focus Strategies
What could you model to help students get through the difficult parts of the lesson?

21
Lesson Plan: Into-Through-and-Beyond
(with instructions)

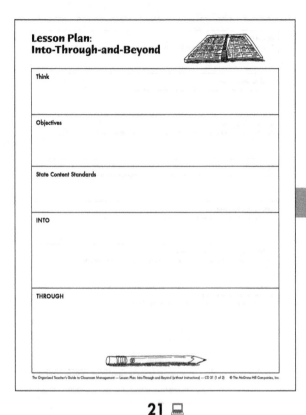

Lesson Plan:
Into-Through-and-Beyond

Think

Objectives

State Content Standards

INTO

THROUGH

21 🖥
Lesson Plan: Into-Through-and-Beyond
(without instructions)

BEYOND

Anticipate Needs

Observe/Clarify/Question

Focus Strategies

21 🖥
Lesson Plan: Into-Through-and-Beyond
(without instructions)

22
Library Labels

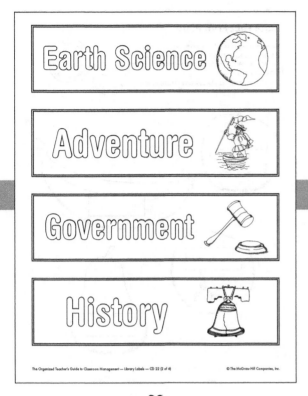

22
Library Labels

22
Library Labels

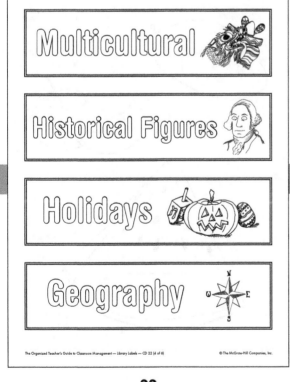

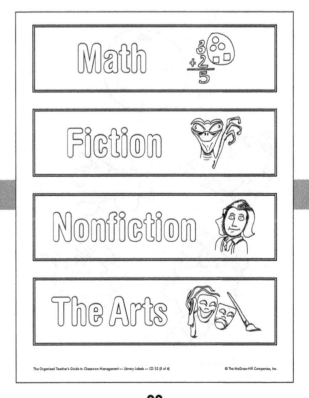

22
Library Labels

22
Library Labels

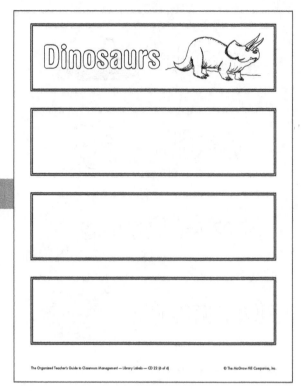

22 🖳
Library Labels

Math Fact Fruit Plate

You will need a paper plate for this activity.

1. Write the numbers 1 through 12 on the pieces of fruit below. Include the math sign (+, −, ×, ÷) that you are working on now.
2. Cut out the pieces of fruit.
3. Starting with the "1" fruit, glue each piece of fruit to the plate as you master the math facts for that number.

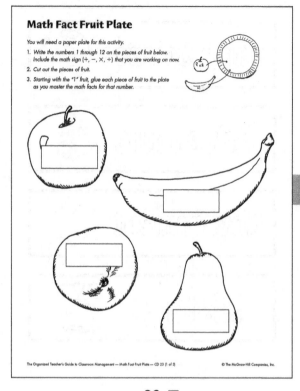

23 🖳
Math Fact Fruit Plate

23 🖳
Math Fact Fruit Plate

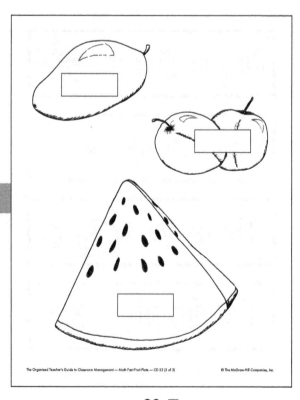

23 🖳
Math Fact Fruit Plate

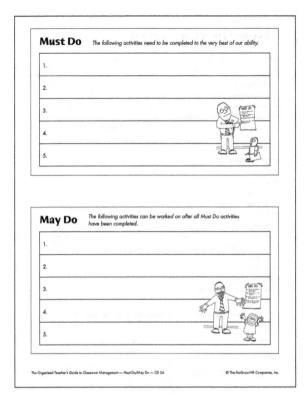

Must Do *The following activities need to be completed to the very best of our ability.*

1.
2.
3.
4.
5.

May Do *The following activities can be worked on after all Must Do activities have been completed.*

1.
2.
3.
4.
5.

24 🖥
Must Do/May Do

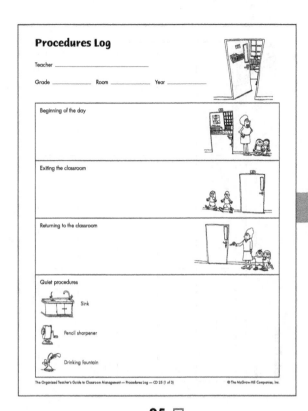

Procedures Log

Teacher _____

Grade _____ Room _____ Year _____

Beginning of the day

Exiting the classroom

Returning to the classroom

Quiet procedures

Sink

Pencil sharpener

Drinking fountain

25 🖥
Procedures Log

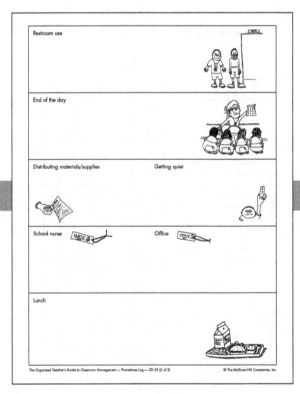

Restroom use

End of the day

Distributing materials/supplies   Getting quiet

School nurse   Office

Lunch

25 🖥
Procedures Log

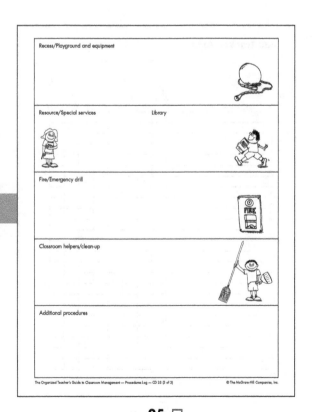

Recess/Playground and equipment

Resource/Special services   Library

Fire/Emergency drill

Classroom helpers/clean-up

Additional procedures

25 🖥
Procedures Log

Rule Planner

Teacher _____

Grade _____ Room _____

Rule	Cause	Effect

26
Rule Planner

Scavenger Hunt Questionnaire

Name _____ Date _____

I found someone who . . .

1. Was born in July: _____
2. Has more than one sibling: _____
3. Likes classical music: _____
4. Has been to Disneyland or Disney World: _____
5. Speaks another language: _____ Which language? _____
6. Likes to swim: _____
7. Likes to paint: _____
8. Is from an ethnic group different from mine: _____
9. Has a pet: _____ What kind? _____
10. Owns an iPod: _____
11. Likes to dance: _____
12. Has traveled out of the state: _____ Where? _____
13. Has been on a cruise: _____ Where? _____
14. Likes Brussels sprouts: _____
15. Plays sports: _____ Which sports? _____
16. Likes Mexican food: _____
17. Dislikes pizza: _____
18. Has or has had braces: _____
19. Has met a movie star: _____ Which star? _____
20. Was born in the state where I live: _____

What do you have in common with your classmates?
I like _____, and so does _____.
Sometimes I _____, and so does _____.
I don't like _____, and neither does _____.
I want _____, and so does _____.

27
Scavenger Hunt Questionnaire

Skill Tracker: Arts

Teacher _____ Room _____ Date _____

Student's Name / Skill/Standard

1.							
2.							
3.							
4.							
5.							
6.							
7.							
8.							
9.							
10.							
11.							
12.							
13.							
14.							
15.							
16.							
17.							
18.							
19.							
20.							
21.							
22.							
23.							
24.							
25.							

28 🖥
Skill Tracker: Arts

Skill Tracker: E.L.D.

Teacher _____ Room _____ Date _____

Student's Name / Skill/Standard

1.							
2.							
3.							
4.							
5.							
6.							
7.							
8.							
9.							
10.							
11.							
12.							
13.							
14.							
15.							
16.							
17.							
18.							
19.							
20.							
21.							
22.							
23.							
24.							
25.							

29 🖥
Skill Tracker: E.L.D.

Skill Tracker: Geography

Teacher _____ Room _____ Date _____

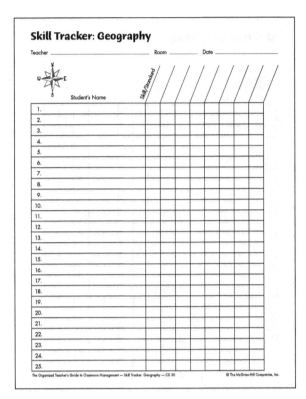

Student's Name	Skill/Standard							
1.								
2.								
3.								
4.								
5.								
6.								
7.								
8.								
9.								
10.								
11.								
12.								
13.								
14.								
15.								
16.								
17.								
18.								
19.								
20.								
21.								
22.								
23.								
24.								
25.								

The Organized Teacher's Guide to Classroom Management — Skill Tracker: Geography — CD 30   © The McGraw-Hill Companies, Inc.

30 💻
Skill Tracker: Geography

Skill Tracker: Health

Teacher _____ Room _____ Date _____

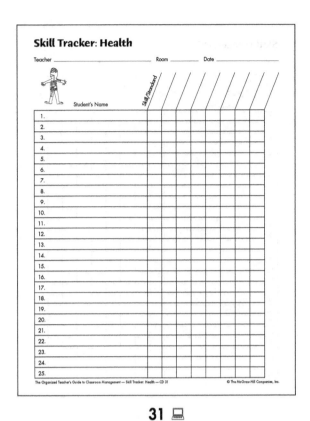

Student's Name	Skill/Standard							
1.								
2.								
3.								
4.								
5.								
6.								
7.								
8.								
9.								
10.								
11.								
12.								
13.								
14.								
15.								
16.								
17.								
18.								
19.								
20.								
21.								
22.								
23.								
24.								
25.								

The Organized Teacher's Guide to Classroom Management — Skill Tracker: Health — CD 31   © The McGraw-Hill Companies, Inc.

31 💻
Skill Tracker: Health

Skill Tracker: Language Arts

Teacher _____ Room _____ Date _____

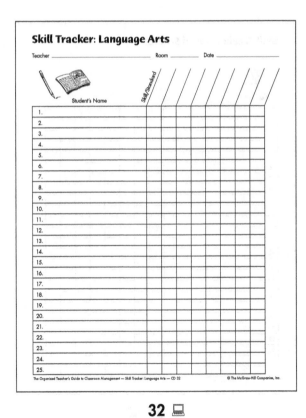

Student's Name	Skill/Standard							
1.								
2.								
3.								
4.								
5.								
6.								
7.								
8.								
9.								
10.								
11.								
12.								
13.								
14.								
15.								
16.								
17.								
18.								
19.								
20.								
21.								
22.								
23.								
24.								
25.								

The Organized Teacher's Guide to Classroom Management — Skill Tracker: Language Arts — CD 32   © The McGraw-Hill Companies, Inc.

32 💻
Skill Tracker: Language Arts

Skill Tracker: Math

Teacher _____ Room _____ Date _____

3 + 2 = 5

Student's Name	Skill/Standard							
1.								
2.								
3.								
4.								
5.								
6.								
7.								
8.								
9.								
10.								
11.								
12.								
13.								
14.								
15.								
16.								
17.								
18.								
19.								
20.								
21.								
22.								
23.								
24.								
25.								

The Organized Teacher's Guide to Classroom Management — Skill Tracker: Math — CD 33   © The McGraw-Hill Companies, Inc.

33 💻
Skill Tracker: Math

Skill Tracker: P.E.

Teacher _____ Room _____ Date _____

Student's Name — Skill/Standard

	1.						
2.						
3.						
4.						
5.						
6.						
7.						
8.						
9.						
10.						
11.						
12.						
13.						
14.						
15.						
16.						
17.						
18.						
19.						
20.						
21.						
22.						
23.						
24.						
25.						

34 💻
Skill Tracker: P.E.

Skill Tracker: Reading

Teacher _____ Room _____ Date _____

Student's Name — Skill/Standard

1.						
2.						
3.						
4.						
5.						
6.						
7.						
8.						
9.						
10.						
11.						
12.						
13.						
14.						
15.						
16.						
17.						
18.						
19.						
20.						
21.						
22.						
23.						
24.						
25.						

35 💻
Skill Tracker: Reading

Skill Tracker: Science

Teacher _____ Room _____ Date _____

Student's Name — Skill/Standard

1.						
2.						
3.						
4.						
5.						
6.						
7.						
8.						
9.						
10.						
11.						
12.						
13.						
14.						
15.						
16.						
17.						
18.						
19.						
20.						
21.						
22.						
23.						
24.						
25.						

36 💻
Skill Tracker: Science

Skill Tracker: Social Studies

Teacher _____ Room _____ Date _____

Student's Name — Skill/Standard

1.						
2.						
3.						
4.						
5.						
6.						
7.						
8.						
9.						
10.						
11.						
12.						
13.						
14.						
15.						
16.						
17.						
18.						
19.						
20.						
21.						
22.						
23.						
24.						
25.						

37 💻
Skill Tracker: Social Studies

Skill Tracker: Writing

Teacher _____ Room _____ Date _____

	Student's Name	Skill/Standard							
1.									
2.									
3.									
4.									
5.									
6.									
7.									
8.									
9.									
10.									
11.									
12.									
13.									
14.									
15.									
16.									
17.									
18.									
19.									
20.									
21.									
22.									
23.									
24.									
25.									

The Organized Teacher's Guide to Classroom Management — Skill Tracker: Writing — CD 38   © The McGraw-Hill Companies, Inc.

38 🖥
Skill Tracker: Writing

Student Contact Information

Teacher _____

Grade _____ Room _____ Year _____

	Student's Name	Guardian	Cell Phone	E-Mail
1.				
2.				
3.				
4.				
5.				
6.				
7.				
8.				
9.				
10.				
11.				
12.				
13.				
14.				
15.				
16.				
17.				
18.				
19.				
20.				
21.				
22.				
23.				
24.				
25.				

The Organized Teacher's Guide to Classroom Management — Student Contact Information — CD 39   © The McGraw-Hill Companies, Inc.

39 🖥
Student Contact Information

Student Interest Survey

Name _____ Age _____

Three things I like to do in my spare time:

1. _____
2. _____
3. _____

My favorite things:

Favorite video game _____   Favorite sport _____

Favorite food _____   Favorite candy _____

Favorite TV show _____   Favorite movie _____

Favorite actor _____   Favorite singer _____

Favorite website _____   Favorite radio station _____

Favorite book I've read _____

Favorite subject in school _____

Best memory of school _____

When I grow up, I would like to be _____

How I describe myself:

Adjective _____

Verb _____

Noun _____

Two of my friends are _____ and _____ .

These things are important to me: _____

The Organized Teacher's Guide to Classroom Management — Student Interest Survey — CD 40   © The McGraw-Hill Companies, Inc.

40
Student Interest Survey

Student Name Cards

These cards can be used to call on students in class.

Record one student's name on each card below, then print the sheet on card stock.

The Organized Teacher's Guide to Classroom Management — Student Name Cards — CD 41   © The McGraw-Hill Companies, Inc.

41 🖥
Student Name Cards

Student Name Strips

These cards can be used to call on students in class.
Record one student's name on each strip below, then print the sheet on card stock.

42 🖥
Student Name Strips

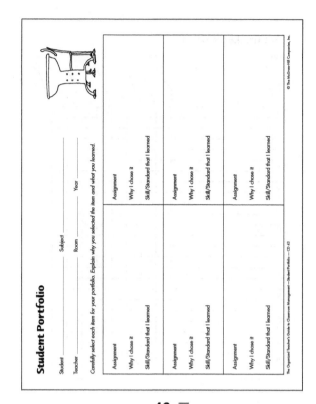

Student Portfolio

Student _____ Subject _____
Teacher _____ Room _____ Year _____

Carefully select each item for your portfolio. Explain why you selected the item and what you learned.

Assignment

Why I chose it

Skill/Standard that I learned

43 🖥
Student Portfolio

Student Question Forms

Write key words or skills from the current unit on the top section below, and attach it to the outside of a manila envelope. Place completed Student Question forms inside the envelope.

Unit/Chapter

Key words/skills

Write a question or problem relating to this unit on the front of your Student Question form. Write your answer on the back. Place your form in the envelope and pass it to the next student.

Student Question
Write your question or problem below. Write your answer on the back. Place the form in the envelope and pass it to the next student.

Name _____ Date _____

Student Question
Write your question or problem below. Write your answer on the back. Place the form in the envelope and pass it to the next student.

Name _____ Date _____

Student Question
Write your question or problem below. Write your answer on the back. Place the form in the envelope and pass it to the next student.

Name _____ Date _____

44 🖥
Student Question Forms

Student Question
Write your question or problem below. Write your answer on the back. Place the form in the envelope and pass it to the next student.

Name _____ Date _____

Student Question
Write your question or problem below. Write your answer on the back. Place the form in the envelope and pass it to the next student.

Name _____ Date _____

Student Question
Write your question or problem below. Write your answer on the back. Place the form in the envelope and pass it to the next student.

Name _____ Date _____

Student Question
Write your question or problem below. Write your answer on the back. Place the form in the envelope and pass it to the next student.

Name _____ Date _____

44
Student Question Forms

Student Reponse Forms

Write a question about a learned or will-learn activity on the top section below, and attach it to the outside of a manila envelope. Place completed Student Response forms inside the envelope.

Question

Write your response to this question on a Student Response form. You may write on the front and back of the form. Place your form in the envelope and pass it to the next student.

Student Response

Write your response below. Place the form in the envelope and pass it to the next student.

Name _____ Date _____

Student Response

Write your response below. Place the form in the envelope and pass it to the next student.

Name _____ Date _____

Student Response

Write your response below. Place the form in the envelope and pass it to the next student.

Name _____ Date _____

The Organized Teacher's Guide to Classroom Management — Student Response Forms — CD 45 (1 of 2)   © The McGraw-Hill Companies, Inc.

45 💻
Student Response Forms

Student Response

Write your response below. Place the form in the envelope and pass it to the next student.

Name _____ Date _____

Student Response

Write your response below. Place the form in the envelope and pass it to the next student.

Name _____ Date _____

Student Response

Write your response below. Place the form in the envelope and pass it to the next student.

Name _____ Date _____

Student Response

Write your response below. Place the form in the envelope and pass it to the next student.

Name _____ Date _____

The Organized Teacher's Guide to Classroom Management — Student Question Forms — CD 45 (2 of 2)   © The McGraw-Hill Companies, Inc.

45
Student Response Forms

Textbook Inventory

Teacher _____

Grade _____ Room _____

Subject/Curricular area Teacher's edition/manual Student editions Additional resources	Subject/Curricular area Teacher's edition/manual Student editions Additional resources
Subject/Curricular area Teacher's edition/manual Student editions Additional resources	Subject/Curricular area Teacher's edition/manual Student editions Additional resources
Subject/Curricular area Teacher's edition/manual Student editions Additional resources	Subject/Curricular area Teacher's edition/manual Student editions Additional resources

The Organized Teacher's Guide to Classroom Management — Textbook Inventory — CD 46   © The McGraw-Hill Companies, Inc.

46 💻
Textbook Inventory

Textbook Sign-Out Sheet

Subject _____

Teacher _____ Room _____

Student's Name	Book Number	Sign-Out Date	Sign-In Date
1.			
2.			
3.			
4.			
5.			
6.			
7.			
8.			
9.			
10.			
11.			
12.			
13.			
14.			
15.			
16.			
17.			
18.			
19.			
20.			
21.			
22.			
23.			
24.			
25.			

The Organized Teacher's Guide to Classroom Management — Textbook Sign-Out Sheet — CD 47   © The McGraw-Hill Companies, Inc.

47 💻
Textbook Sign-Out Sheet

Time Capsule

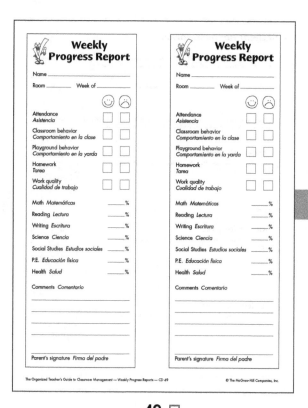

This time capsule was established on _____
Date (month, day, year)

It belongs to _____
Student's name

Inventory

Check-Off	Contents

48 🖥
Time Capsule

Weekly Progress Report

Name _____
Room _____ Week of _____

	☺	☹
Attendance / *Asistencia*	☐	☐
Classroom behavior / *Comportamiento en la clase*	☐	☐
Playground behavior / *Comportamiento en la yarda*	☐	☐
Homework / *Tarea*	☐	☐
Work quality / *Cualidad de trabajo*	☐	☐

Math *Matemáticas* _____%
Reading *Lectura* _____%
Writing *Escritura* _____%
Science *Ciencia* _____%
Social Studies *Estudios sociales* _____%
P.E. *Educación física* _____%
Health *Salud* _____%

Comments *Comentario*
_____
_____
_____
_____

Parent's signature *Firma del padre*

Weekly Progress Report

Name _____
Room _____ Week of _____

	☺	☹
Attendance / *Asistencia*	☐	☐
Classroom behavior / *Comportamiento en la clase*	☐	☐
Playground behavior / *Comportamiento en la yarda*	☐	☐
Homework / *Tarea*	☐	☐
Work quality / *Cualidad de trabajo*	☐	☐

Math *Matemáticas* _____%
Reading *Lectura* _____%
Writing *Escritura* _____%
Science *Ciencia* _____%
Social Studies *Estudios sociales* _____%
P.E. *Educación física* _____%
Health *Salud* _____%

Comments *Comentario*
_____
_____
_____
_____

Parent's signature *Firma del padre*

49 🖥
Weekly Progress Reports

Writing Process Folder

Name _____

Writing Assignment	Genre	Date

Pre-Write ⇨ Draft ⇨ Edit/Revise ⇨ Proofread ⇨ Publish

Share/Reflect

50
Writing Process Folder

Pre-Write

51
Writing Process Tracker

Draft

51

Writing Process Tracker

Edit/Revise

51

Writing Process Tracker

Proofread

51

Writing Process Tracker

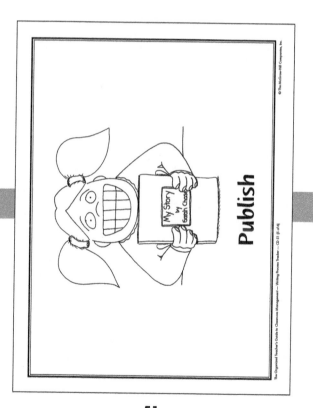

Publish

51

Writing Process Tracker

51
Writing Process Tracker

The Organized Teacher's Guide to Classroom Management — Writing Process Tracker — CD-51 (6 of 6)

© The McGraw-Hill Companies, Inc.

Share/Reflect

Index

CD templates are indicated in Capital and Small Capital Letters; *template numbers are in square brackets.*